Global Bondage

The U.N.
Plan to Rule
the
World

by Cliff Kincaid

Huntington House Publishers

Huntington House Publishers
P.O. Box 53788
Lafayette, Louisiana 70505

Library of Congress Card Catalog Number 95-77354
ISBN 1-56384-103-7

Printed in the U.S.A.

Graphics by Jaynell Trosclair

Contents

The U.N.

The World Government

The most important battle in American history is now taking place. In 1995—the fiftieth anniversary of the founding of the United Nations (U.N.)—Americans are deciding whether they will continue on the road to a world government dominated by foreign and hostile interests or assert the principles of American sovereignty. At stake is nothing less than America as generations have known it.

Today, however, we have already witnessed the disgraceful spectacle of American troops dying in military operations outside of the control of our own elected officials which may one day threaten our own citizens. These U.N. "peacekeeping operations," directed by the U.N. itself, feature American soldiers in such places as Somalia and Haiti as blue-helmeted "United Nations fighting persons" who lose their status as American POW/MIAs when captured or killed.

Pres. Bill Clinton, the leading proponent of these U.N. military operations, claims those opposed to his foreign and defense policies are practicing a "new form of isolationism." But, Clinton, who organized demonstrations against his own country on foreign soil and who traveled throughout the Communist bloc during the Vietnam War, is practicing a form of "internationalism" that deliberately diminishes America's standing in the world.

Clinton, who avoided the Vietnam War draft and let someone else go in his place, came into office at a time when the Cold War had ended and America could have reasserted itself as the leader of the entire world. Instead, under Clinton's leadership, America has become subservient to the U.N., has forged a military "partnership" with the remnants of the Soviet Union, and has permitted Russia to use the U.N. as cover to wage war against its own people. Incredibly, U.S. troops have even participated in peacekeeping operations with Russian military forces. (See chapter 6.)

At this crossroads in American history, some influential policy- and opinion-makers are now openly calling on the American people to voluntarily sacrifice the power to guide our own destiny as a nation. Leslie Gelb, a former *New York Times* reporter and now president of the influential Council on Foreign Relations, says, "The very long process of shaping a more effective and responsible United Nations must begin. This will require some sacrifices of sovereignty."[1]

It's rare when U.N. proponents admit that their plans involve surrendering American independence. However, the goal of world government was the openly announced objective of the March 1995 U.N.-sponsored World Summit for Social Development in Copenhagen, Denmark.

Described in the press as just a worthwhile event designed to eradicate poverty, the U.N. Development Program (UNDP)—the main sponsor—had issued a "Human Development Report" openly calling for "world government" in a featured article written by Nobel Prize-winning economist Jan Tinbergen, who declared, "Mankind's problems can no longer be solved by national governments. What is needed is a World Government. This can best be achieved by strengthening the United Nations system." In addition to the world army already coming into existence (see chapter 2), he urged establishment of a World Ministry of Agriculture, a World Ministry of Industry, a World Ministry of Social Affairs, and a World Police.

On top of the many corrupt layers of bureaucracy that already make up the U.N. system, the UNDP report urged member U.N. states to strengthen the world body by establishing another level, an "Economic Security Council," to manage a "global human security fund" financed by global taxation to the tune of $1.5 trillion over five years. The revenues were to come from the imposition of international taxes and cutbacks in military spending. One such proposal, outlined in the UNDP report, was the "Tobin tax" on international currency transactions, named after 1981 Nobel Prize-winning economist James Tobin.[2] The Clinton administration gave tacit support to these schemes by sending Vice President Gore and Mrs. Clinton to the event.

A scheme of global taxation was not officially adopted at the world summit. The U.N. planners decided to put it off for the time being. However, the UNDP has since published an article in its magazine advocating a new variation on the Tobin tax.[3] It is clear that the U.N. will return to the idea in future conferences because of the perceived need to make the U.N. a financially independent organization that does not have to seek "contributions" from member countries.

If the American people were fully informed that international bureaucrats were plotting at taxpayer expense to raise our taxes even further (since Americans pay about one-third of U.N. costs), there might be revolution in the streets. After all, Americans are

already overtaxed, paying about 40 percent of their
income in taxes to various levels of government in the
United States. Yet, they don't feel safe in their neigh-
borhoods, their children aren't educated properly in
the public schools, and the federal government seems
unable to balance its budget or do anything about
massive trade deficits that drain America's wealth away
to predatory trade partners such as Japan.

From the U.N. perspective, global taxes are needed
because of "global problems" that require "global
solutions." If there was life on other planets, they
would almost certainly support a galactic form of
government. The fallacy in this socialistic reasoning is
an old one. The more complex the society (or the
world), they argue, the more government control we
need. In fact, it is wiser under these circumstances to
delegate and decentralize power, to rely on human
beings to solve their own problems. Incentive and
individual responsibility are stifled in larger organizations. But, the approach of individual freedom and
responsibility doesn't give bureaucrats more and more
power to run our lives.

Currently, the U.N. emphasizes several good-sound-
ing causes to increase its power. One is environmental
protection. It is significant that the head of the UNDP,
the agency pushing global taxes, is a Clinton appoin-
tee, an American named James Gustave Speth, who
helped establish the radical environmental group
known as the Natural Resources Defense Council
(NRDC). The NRDC's success in the United States
helps us understand one way in which the U.N. works
on an international level. The NRDC specializes in
scare campaigns designed to increase government regulation and control of American industry (and the taxes
necessary to make that possible) in the name of saving
the environment. For instance, the NRDC, working
with influential media organizations, was responsible

for the 1989 national scare campaign over the chemical Alar on apples and apple products. The NRDC called the chemical, a preservative used to improve the shelf life of apples, a carcinogen. The intent was to force government agencies, which deemed the chemical essentially harmless to humans, to ban it. In the end, the national hysteria resulted in the loss of hundreds of millions of dollars to apple farmers and the maker of Alar took it off the market voluntarily. Ironically, the NRDC campaign had the effect of causing millions of Americans to refrain from eating apples and apple products, which are effective in fighting cancer.

The U.N. performs much the same way on an international basis by holding events such as the 1992 Earth Summit, which Vice President Gore attended and was designed to create worldwide hysteria over how nations of the world, led by the United States, were supposedly damaging the environment of the planet through industrial activity and economic growth. In this regard, the U.N. embraces every scare campaign about the environment, ranging from the alleged dangers of global warming to protecting the ozone layer. Under its sponsorship, the United States and other nations have adopted treaties and agreements that attempt, through complicated rules and regulations (enforced by government bureaucracies and supported by higher and higher taxes), to reduce emissions of substances, chemicals or gasses that are said to be causing environmental problems. A great deal of evidence has been produced suggesting the theories underpinning these actions are just plain wrong. In any case, there seems to be no serious thought given to why the U.N., a horribly mismanaged bureaucracy with tremendous waste, fraud, and abuse, should be set up as some kind of international arbiter of technological and scientific progress. The former

Soviet Union, perhaps the most polluted country in the world, is a prime example of what happens when centralized government attempts to regulate the environment.

Another favorite cause of the U.N. is trade liberalization—the reduction of trade barriers between nations. Here, some conservatives have fallen for the bait. On the face of it, "free trade" seems to run counter to the notion of big government. However, "free trade" as envisioned by the U.N. involves giving international bureaucracies the power to manage trade relations between states and punish those who violate the rules. The General Agreement on Tariffs and Trade (GATT), which has now been supplanted by the World Trade Organization (WTO), is an official part of the U.N. system today.

Many conservatives supported the WTO, despite their misgivings over its impact on American sovereignty. House Speaker Newt Gingrich, for one, said he was worried that the WTO, where the United States has no veto power, would become a "Third world-dominated, dictatorship-dominated system," adding, "I'm for world trade, but I'm against world government." Even after endorsing it, Gingrich called the WTO "not just another trade agreement" but something which will result in "a very big transfer of power."[4]

Gingrich's fears are well-grounded. Back in 1974, Richard Gardner, a deputy assistant secretary of state for International Organization Affairs in the Kennedy and Johnson administrations, wrote a very revealing article entitled "The Hard Road to World Order" in the Council on Foreign Relations journal *Foreign Affairs*. Gardner predicted that new GATT arrangements and procedures would amount to "an end-run around national sovereignty, eroding it piece by piece, [which] will accomplish much more than the old-fashioned frontal assault." He said the new GATT would "subject countries to an unprecedented degree of international surveillance over up to now sacrosanct 'domestic' policies."[5]

After surveying areas in which the U.N. was even then expanding its power and authority, including the field of U.N. peacekeeping, Gardner went on to make this revealing statement:

> Thus, while we will not see "world government" in the old-fashioned sense of a single all-embracing global authority, key elements of planetary planning and planetary management will come about on those very specific problems where the facts of interdependence force nations, in their enlightened self-interest, to abandon unilateral decision-making in favor of multilateral processes.[6]

The other problem with free trade, as defined by the U.N., is that it provides perfect cover for drug trafficking and drug-money laundering. The North American Free Trade Agreement (NAFTA)—a pact to spur business activity by lowering trade barriers and reducing border inspections between the United States, Canada, and Mexico—was seen by U.S. intelligence officials as facilitating drug trafficking into the United States from Mexico, a country almost as corrupt as Colombia.[7]

Before NAFTA, between 50 to 70 percent of the cocaine smuggled into the United States from countries such as Colombia came through Mexico. After NAFTA, one group called the American Coalition for Competitive Trade reported that an explosion of illegal drugs into the United States had become a reality and that "tons of cocaine stream across the Mexican border to be dumped on our schoolyards every day."[8]

The worst, however, may be yet to come. In concert with the Clinton administration, the U.N. appears to be moving to embrace the legalization of dangerous mind-altering substances as part of a new "international approach" to the drug problem. At first glance, legalization seems like a libertarian proposal that runs counter to the idea of bigger government which the U.N. embraces. Like free trade, however, legalization of drugs would entail a massive expansion of government power. The Lucis Trust, a pro-U.N. organization on the roster of the U.N. Economic and Social Council, described this option in a newsletter on the "Global Crisis" of illegal drugs. It noted:

> There are pressures in many countries to decriminalize illegal drugs so that addicts receive rehabilitative treatment, and not be branded as criminals. One senior British police officer recently suggested that currently illicit drugs could be sold by pharmacists as part of a government monopoly with marketing and promotion prohibited. However, this strategy would only work if "implemented simultaneously in all major countries."[9]

The key phrases are "government monopoly" and "implemented simultaneously in all major countries." Dr. Joycelyn Elders, who served as President Clinton's surgeon general, saw legalization in much the same way. She had suggested on several occasions that dangerous drugs be legalized. However, "When we say 'legalize,'" she told *USA Weekend Magazine*, "I'm really talking about *control* (emphasis added). That we have doctors or clinics set up where addicts can get their drugs free, or pay $1."[10]

Viewed in this context, the strategy of legalization is designed to increase the power of government to control people by operating clinics where substances like marijuana, cocaine, and even heroin are dispensed. On an international level, it means increasing the power of national governments acting in coordination with the U.N. to "control" the drug trade.

Is there any reason to believe the U.N. is moving down this road? When Stephanie Haynes, president of Drug Watch International, received an advance copy of an agenda for a 1994 conference of the U.N. Drug Control Program (UNDCP) in Bangkok, Thailand, she was astounded:

> The overall "theme" of the conference, as reflected in the choice of workshop topics, seems to run counter to U.N. policies, and in particular to the 1992 report of the International Narcotics Control Board which stated that there are "no viable alternatives to traditional drug abuse control efforts" and that legalization is not an answer to the drug abuse problem. The emphasis of the conference workshops appears to be less on demand reduction and prevention, and more on treatment, public health issues, and alternatives to demand reduction. The public health approach, as you may know, is a key strategy of "harm reduction" and pro-drug advocates.[11]

Indeed, the proposed solution, called *harm-reduction* by its advocates, involves the government giving drugs and even free needles away to drug addicts supposedly to control the problem. This approach is in sharp contrast to demand reduction and prevention, aimed at discouraging drug use through legal and educational efforts.

In Europe, some nations are trying the harm-reduction approach. For instance, young people in Holland can use marijuana in coffee houses, while heroin and cocaine addicts can use or abuse their drugs on public streets or in public bathrooms, while police simply congregate nearby and look the other way. Britain has a so-called heroin maintenance program where addicts maintain their habits at taxpayer expense. In Zurich, Switzerland, however, the harm-reduction experiment known as Needle Park, an area set aside for users, was an utter disaster. Nearby residents were disgusted by the filth and danger. Addicts frequently wandered away, throwing syringes, blood-soaked tissues and even condoms on children's playgrounds. It took a year and seven hundred thousand dollars to clean up and restore the area, including replacing topsoil polluted by used syringes and human waste.

Why, then, is there some support in the United States for a harm-reduction approach? Some conservatives have fallen for it because they think there have been too many government excesses in the war on drugs. They think legalization could somehow reduce the violence associated with the procurement and use of illegal substances. They ignore the fact that even the staunch proponents of legalization acknowledge that drugs could not be legal for children and, therefore, there would be a continuing need for law enforcement activity to protect them. In addition, law enforcement would be necessary to prevent a black market from developing for drugs different or stronger than the government-approved variety. In other words, legalization could easily result in the worst of both worlds—more drug use and more drug-related violence.

A critical fact is that most support for harm-reduction or legalization comes from groups whose leaders use or abuse drugs. This should not be too surprising. After all, there are plenty of weak-willed people who fall victim to the drug scourge. Drugs are a terrible temptation to many. That's why we have a drug problem. For example, the head of the National Organization for the Reform of Marijuana Laws (NORML),

Richard Cowan, is a proud daily marijuana smoker who enjoys getting stoned. Some of the people involved in the Drug Policy Foundation, a group whose leadership supports legalization, have been users as well. There is a magazine called *High Times* that exists for these people which glamorizes drug use. These people want drugs legalized so they can use them openly and get them cheaper, preferably from government stores. The more honest pro-drug advocates admit that legalization, by making drugs more available and morally acceptable, would increase drug use.

Drug trafficking into the United States, by countries such as Colombia and Mexico, should be viewed as a literal invasion requiring a national security response. While U.S. law enforcement personnel have overstepped their legal authority on occasion in the war on drugs, America hardly has a "tough law and order" approach to the problem. Most first time users in the United States are *not* arrested and sent to prison. A truly tough approach is evident in places like Singapore, where drug dealers are hanged. If America were really tough on drugs, there would be widespread drug testing in American society. But, thanks to lawyers from the ACLU, who sue to prevent such tests on grounds of invasion of privacy, there is not. The ACLU is also on record in favor of legalizing drugs.[12]

Under a U.N.-sponsored plan to legalize drugs on a worldwide basis, drug trafficking countries such as Colombia or Mexico would become "respectable." Notorious drug traffickers and their bankers would be transformed into legitimate businessmen. Previously illegal entities would suddenly become legal under the supervision of national governments and the U.N. Indeed, one way the U.N. could end up voting for legalization is for countries complicit in narcotics trafficking to combine their forces together with other nations, especially in Europe, which are already moving toward a more liberal policy on drugs. The European Parliamentary Commission on Civil Liberties and Internal Affairs reportedly voted in late January 1995 to decriminalize marijuana.[13] A similar vote by the full European Parliament could follow.

Significantly, when Conrad K. Harper, legal adviser in Clinton's Department of State, announced that the United States supported creation of a U.N.-sponsored International Criminal Court, he went out of his way to say that the Clinton administration "does not support including drug-related crimes within the court's jurisdiction." Incredibly, he said, "We do not believe that the United Nations Convention Against Illicit Traffic in Narcotics Drugs and Psychotropic Substances of 1988 provides the level of specificity needed to form the basis of criminal charges." Instead, Harper said the United States wants the court to focus on such concerns as "war crimes, crimes against humanity and genocide."[14]

Aware that such a position could imply a soft-on-drugs attitude, Harper insisted, "No one can doubt the commitment of my government to combating terrorism and drug trafficking." In fact, Clinton's drug policies have been strongly attacked, with former Drug Enforcement administration chief Robert Bonner, who served under Presidents Bush and Clinton, saying "there has been a near total absence of Presidential leadership" by Clinton on the issue.[15]

A former marijuana user who joked about not inhaling, Clinton, as Arkansas governor, pardoned a convicted cocaine trafficker named Dan Lasater, who had been a friend and campaign contributor. Investigations into the Clintons' role in the Whitewater real estate deal and Madison Guaranty Savings & Loan have led to the Arab-owned Bank of Credit and Commerce International (BCCI), accused of involvement with terrorists and arms- and drug-traffickers BCCI is believed to have been secretly working to acquire important segments of the U.S. banking industry.

Clinton came into office promising appointment of a cabinet-level drug czar who would intensify the war on drugs. But, one of his first actions was to slash the staff of the White House Office of National Drug Control Policy by 84 percent, leaving only twenty-five people to coordinate the effort. Then he appointed people like Dr. Elders to his administration and kept her on until she made one embarrassing comment too many.

The difference is striking. Under Presidents Reagan and Bush, the emphasis was put on reducing both the supply of drugs and demand for them. The result was that by the time Clinton took office, the number of current users of drugs was half of what it was in 1979, the peak period. Under Clinton, however, both the supply of and demand for drugs have increased. In addition, there has been a reemergence of pro-drug messages in music and films coming out of Hollywood, a key source of Democratic party and Clinton campaign funds. As a consequence, drug use among teen-agers has been going up since Clinton took office. For example, a 1994 U.S. government survey found that, among high school seniors, 30.7 percent had tried marijuana at least once in the past year, compared to only 21.9 percent of 1992 seniors.[16] And, many who try marijuana go on to cocaine. If these trends of marijuana use continue, the Center on Addiction and Substance Abuse at Columbia University warns that 820,000 more of these children will try cocaine, and about fifty-eight thousand of them will become regular users and addicts.

With the drug problem growing at all levels, the Clinton administration might try to claim that, while it wouldn't try to implement decriminalization or legalization on its own, international pressure was forcing it to try this new policy of *harm-reduction* in concert with other nations acting through the U.N. The scourge of international narcotics trafficking, which has a historical Communist component (see chapter 6), could be just the crisis the U.N. needs to move into a more expansive phase, perhaps even into world government.

One thing the pro-drug movement needs, however, is legitimacy. And, it appears to have found that in the person of financier and investor George Soros, a man born in Budapest, Hungary, in 1930 who emigrated to England in 1947 and graduated from the London School of Economics in 1952. He moved to the United States in 1956.

Soros holds the distinction of being "the first person in history to earn a 10-figure salary. His $1.1 billion paycheck [in 1994] exceeds the gross domestic product of at least 42 countries in the United Nations."[17] Soros is the manager of the $10 billion Quantum Fund, which is registered offshore and closed to U.S. citizens and residents. He made much of his money during the 1980s, the so-called "decade of greed" engineered by Presidents Reagan and Bush, but is nevertheless a major financial backer of Bill Clinton and the Democratic party. Soros contributed to the Clinton presidential campaign in 1992 and made a twenty thousand dollar contribution to the Democratic National Committee.

But, the ironies don't end there. His goal, he says, is to promote "open societies" and, toward that end, he operates a network of foundations in twenty-four countries throughout Central and Eastern Europe and the former Soviet Union, as well as South Africa and the United States. However, his choice for president of his Open Society Institute (OSI) in the United States was Aryeh Neier, former national director of the ACLU.

It was through the OSI that Soros announced on 11 July 1994 that he was providing $6 million to the Drug Policy Foundation (DPF). Speaking for Soros, Neier said,

> George Soros does not believe that the drug war makes any sense from an economic standpoint. The current policy is wasteful and it promotes crime and disease. From every standpoint it is a failure. We believe that it is urgent that alternative approaches be explored. DPF is an essential voice promoting alternative approaches that will reduce the damage done by the drug trade and by the methods currently used to combat the traffic in drugs.[18]

Soros' personal views on the moral, as opposed to economic, dimensions of the drug problem are not known. He has already been brought before Congress to testify about his involvement in controversial financial dealings known as "derivatives." Perhaps he ought to be questioned about his role as the leading funder of the drug legalization movement. The authoritative *Drug Policy Report* says that Soros is so committed to the movement that he hosted a "private dinner" on the matter at his New York home on 8 December 1994, for forty of his friends. One participant called it a "propaganda session," during which four speakers argued that harm-reduction was the wave of the future and that drug legalization has been successful abroad and "would be good" for the United States. The speakers included Ethan Nadelmann, director of the Soros-supported Lindesmith center, and Mathea Falco, president of Drug Strategies, another group that has received Soros money.[19]

Perhaps Soros ought to be questioned as well about his purchase of a 9 percent stake in Banco de Colombia, the second largest bank in Colombia. In 1990, the

Banco de Colombia in Panama City was accused by
the U.S. Drug Enforcement Agency (DEA) of participating in a drug money-laundering scheme that involved transfers of funds from Colombia to Panama.[20]

Soros bought his interest in the Colombian bank
from Bancol, a firm run by a Cali-based businessman
named Jaime Galinski and his father. They bought the
bank in January 1994, with Jaime Galinski saying it
was his intention to strengthen its international operations in Panama and Miami and then expand into
Europe.[21] He made the purchase with financial backing from the ING Bank of the Netherlands, whose
name surfaced in connection with the 4th International Conference on Harm Reduction in Rotterdam
in March of 1993. The ING Bank was listed in conference literature as having made a financial donation to
the conference.

All of this might be entirely innocent. But, this
series of connections has aroused official concern. The
other fascinating thing about Soros is that he is a big
backer of the U.N. He was scheduled to be the keynote speaker at the 11 May 1995 conference of the
Business Council for the U.N. World Congress, where
his topic was, "UN Reform: A Vision for the Next
Century." In a 1994 speech, Soros outlined his views
about the world body:

> Frankly, we are all disillusioned with the United
> Nations. Fifty years ago, young people were
> inspired by it; that is not the case today. But
> we must overcome our reluctance and revive
> our interest. It is clear that the United Nations
> will require a thorough overhaul. What better
> occasion than the fiftieth anniversary? I don't
> quite know how to do it, but I should like to
> devote myself to the reform and revitalization
> of the U.N. and I invite you to join me in the
> effort.[22]

It remains to be seen if any proposed overhaul of the world body includes a shift toward active support of drug legalization. Ironically, Soros could be just the one to volunteer some of his wealth—by endorsing the global tax on the international currency dealings he and others like him engage in—in order to create the new permanent structures that are needed to help the U.N. "control" the problem.

As these events of earth-shattering importance unfold before us, the super-rich broadcaster Ted Turner has emerged as another key player in the U.N.'s game plan. Turner's TBS Superstation achieved notoriety on the drug issue when it broadcast a Network Earth program in April of 1994 that proposed the use of hemp—the plant from which marijuana is derived—for clothing, medicine and even food. *High Times* hailed the program as a breakthrough for the drug culture.

Turner, a one-time conservative, emerged in the 1980s as a propagandist for the Soviet Union, airing no fewer than a dozen films trying to discredit the notion that the Communist regime in Moscow was a national security threat to the United States. One documentary titled "Portrait of the Soviet Union" was described by Turner himself as saying "good things" about the Communist state. Turner even formed a group, the Better World Society, including Soviet Communist party official Georgi Arbatov on its board.[23]

At the same time, Turner got involved in the population control movement, serving on the advisory committee of the Population Institute and airing a documentary on the "global family." At one point, Turner said that one country "doing a good job" of getting its population "under control" was Communist China, whose program includes forced abortion, sterilization and infanticide. Turner's Better World Society gave an award to the U.N. Fund for Popula-

tion Activities (UNFPA), now known as just the U.N.
Population Fund, which supports the China program.[24]
Currently, Turner's networks are part of the so-
called One World Group, a global consortium of broad-
casters who have committed themselves to propagan-
dizing on behalf of the U.N.[25] Turner was the scheduled speaker at a 19 April 1995, event on media coverage of the U.N. sponsored by the U.N. Association
of the U.S. and the U.N. Correspondents Association,
in cooperation with the Columbia School of Journal-
ism (which graduates many influential American journalists), the Committee to Protect Journalists, and the
Freedom Forum Media Studies Center. According to
one report, Turner has

> approved a policy decision to treat all major
> UN conferences "not as isolated events but as
> part of a wider continuum stretching from the
> 1992 Earth Summit, through to the fiftieth
> anniversary of the United Nations." This will
> mean a range of CNN programmes preceding
> and during each conference.[26]

In connection with the Earth Summit, Turner aired
One Child/One Voice, a program described by the
Media Research Center as an attempt to frighten children through "chicken little" theories about environmental problems. To coincide with the September 1994
U.N.-sponsored International Conference on Population and Development, an event promoting abortion
as a form of population control, Turner's TBS
Superstation aired a series of programs under the title
of "People Count," while his CNN broadcast a "Beyond the Numbers" show. The "People Count" series
was hosted by Turner's wife, Jane Fonda, perhaps best
known as a supporter of Communist Hanoi during
the Vietnam War but who is (like her husband) a
"Special Goodwill Ambassador" to the U.N. Popula-

tion Fund. In addition, Turner continues to air his cartoon show, "Captain Planet," in which the superheroes, acting in service to the spirit of Mother Earth, Gaia, impart propaganda messages to small children, such as the need to protect animals through the Endangered Species Act by throwing people out of work.

But, Turner won't be alone in his U.N. cheerleading during the world body's fiftieth anniversary. The taxpayer-funded Public Broadcasting Service (PBS) is planning to air special episodes of "Sesame Street," the popular children's show, to celebrate the U.N.'s "50th Birthday" during the week of 24 October 1995. These programs, according to the U.N. itself, are designed "to reach the pre-school audience." "Sesame Street" characters such as Big Bird were being scheduled for a public appearance at the U.N.[27]

Unfortunately, many adults in recent years have also bought into the notion of world government, having been conditioned by popular futurists into thinking it is inevitable and even worthwhile. These "thinkers" say the trend is away from the preservation of nation-states such as the United States. For example, Alvin Toffler, author of the bestseller *Future Shock*, says the emerging "Third Wave" of human history means there is a different "world system" coming into being:

> The nation-state's role is still further diminished as nations themselves are forced to create supranational agencies. Nation-states fight to retain as much sovereignty and freedom of action as they can. But they are being driven, step by step, to accept new constraints on their independence.[28]

Toffler notes that many European countries have "grudgingly but inevitably" been driven to create a Common Market, a European parliament, and a European monetary system. Interestingly, one of the key bankers advising the European Community on how to prepare for a common currency is Cees Maas, a senior executive of the ING Bank. He says, "The process of European monetary union is under way and is going to happen, and the private sector has to prepare for that."[29]

Clinton's response to all of this is to embrace plans for a "United States of Europe," comparable in economic weight and global influence to the United States.[30] Such a union could very well include Russia.

The European Community was formed to do many good things, such as ending war and fighting unemployment. But, one critic notes that instead of this utopia, Europe today faces extremely high unemployment levels and a war in Bosnia that European nations seem unable to stop.[31] And, plans for a common currency are not going as planned either. Britain and Denmark have reserved the right to opt-out.

Toffler, despite his reputation as a forward thinker, did not seem certain exactly what role the U.N. might play in this new world system. In 1980, when his book was published, he recognized the U.N. as "ossified," "bureaucratic" and in need of an "overhaul."[32] He also denounced as a "fantasy" and "simplistic" the notion that "a single, centralized World Government" could run human affairs. But what, exactly, does an overhaul mean and when is it supposed to occur? And, what are the new agencies that Toffler says were needed to reorganize human affairs? U.N. proponents will undoubtedly come up with a variety of schemes during this fiftieth anniversary year. Toffler's vagueness suggests that the U.N. could be overhauled to the point of abolition and a new world body established in its place.

Alvin and Heidi Toffler, who have since emerged as key advisers to House Speaker Newt Gingrich, have not fully clarified their controversial views on world government. But, they remain convinced that nation-states are doomed. In their latest book, published by the Progress and Freedom Foundation, a group run by associates of Representative Gingrich, the Tofflers flatly declare that "Nationalism is the ideology of the nation-state, which is a product of the industrial revolution" or second wave. They contend that:

> As economies are transformed by the Third Wave, they are compelled to surrender part of their sovereignty and to accept increasing economic and cultural intrusions from one another. Thus, while poets and intellectuals of economically backward regions write national anthems, poets and intellectuals of Third Wave states sing the virtues of a "borderless" world and "planetary consciousness."[33]

Interestingly, despite their links to Gingrich, the Tofflers singled out Vice President Gore as someone who understands these patterns of historical change and is trying to move the United States in the "right" direction. They refer to him as someone "with one toe wet in the Third Wave."[34] Yet, Gore is an enthusiastic supporter of the U.N. and was a strong booster of the U.N. Earth Summit.

Despite their popularity, the Tofflers' vision of the future is not necessarily the correct one. There is nothing inevitable about it at all. In fact, Dr. Michael Zey, author of *Seizing the Future*, argues that the world is entering the "Macroindustrial" era of biotechnology, space travel and space colonies, supertrains, large scale agricultural production, and even artificial islands to house more people. Zey says that if the United States follows the Toffler notion of becoming the hub of a "third wave" information age, we will have sacrificed our status as an industrial superpower capable

of defending our own interests and even our own
people. The United States, he warns, is at risk of becoming a second- or third-rate power, leaving countries like Japan or Germany to dominate the next
century.

Zey admits he was surprised to learn that the
Tofflers were mentors to Gingrich. He hopes that
Gingrich's support for deregulation and scientific
achievement outweighs his reliance on this husband-
wife team.

He is also pleased that Gingrich has indicated a
desire to reduce U.S. reliance on the U.N., which, Zey
argues, is an impediment to human progress. He notes
that the notion popularized at the Earth Summit about
"sustainable development" translates into government-
imposed limits to economic growth and that Gore is
someone who wants to "save us through a huge national bureaucracy that will oversee internal business
action and cede large amounts of national power to
international bureaucracies that will decide whether
the U.S. economic policy falls within environmental
guidelines."[35]

This effort is misguided, according to Zey, who
argues that economic growth and technological ad-
vancement will not only save people but the environment as well.

One benefit of embracing Zey's vision of the future, in addition to reestablishing America's place in
the world, is that the American people themselves
might rediscover the value of what America has stood
for in the past and what it can accomplish in the
future. It would mean America might be dragged kick-
ing and screaming into the third wave. It might mean
saving American sovereignty.

Even while we work to extricate ourselves from
the U.N., we have to fight schemes to enlarge the

world body. Clinton, for example, is pushing a deadly plan to expand the U.N. Security Council, whose permanent members are the United States, Russia, China, France, and Great Britain, to include Germany and Japan. It is significant that the European Union, which is dominated by Germany, is backing Japan's bid for a permanent seat on the U.N. Security Council.[36]

Some say such expansion would lead to more division at the U.N. But, there's another reason to oppose admission by these two nations, who were enemies of the United States during World War II, and that is that they are believed by some strategic experts to be continuing to pursue historic ambitions of world domination.

Japan's influence over America is a sensitive subject. While Clinton was applauded in April for saying the United States should not apologize for dropping the atomic bombs on Japan that hastened the end of the war, he had previously put pressure on the U.S. Postal Service to drop a World War II commemorative stamp depicting that bombing. His administration was also accused of trying to play down the use of the term *V-J* or Victory over Japan in connection with the anniversary of that event.

It is frequently said about Japan that it is trying to accomplish economically what it failed to do militarily. In an economic version of Pearl Harbor, Japan has relentlessly engaged in predatory trade practices against the United States designed to build up its own industries. America's trade deficits have resulted in the transfer of literally hundreds of billions of dollars to Japan, some of which is plowed back into the United States to buy American property or debt securities, enabling the Japanese to acquire a form of leverage over our economy. These properties include Hollywood film studios and record companies, whose products include violent-oriented and even pro-drug movies and songs. Sony, for example, marketed pro-marijuana rap groups such as Cypress Hill to America's young people, even though then-Sony chairman Akio Morita had co-authored a provocative book, *The Japan That Can Say No*, arguing that America was morally inferior to Japan in part because of our drug problem.

Today, according to William J. Gill, author of *Trade Wars Against America*,

> Our chronic huge trade deficits with Japan [have] fueled the rise of Japanese banks and the relative subsidence of Citibank, Chase Manhattan, Bank of America and other big U.S. banks. Indeed, Bank of America is now a virtual subsidiary of a Japanese bank. Japan dominates the world of finance and the dollar is worth one-fourth of the value it held in 1972.[37]

The United States is also heavily dependent on Germany. In their explosive book, *Selling Our Security*, Martin and Susan Tolchin reported that the U.S. victory in the Persian Gulf War actually underscored our weaknesses:

> The technological superiority that vanquished Iraq and impressed the world owed much of its success to the products of foreign countries: almost all of the optical glass used in reconnaissance satellites came from Germany, gallium-arsenide chips used in radar and satellite receivers from Japan, and five parts of the Abrams tank, including the optics in the gunner's sight and an ingredient in the seal, were made by foreign companies.[38]

During the war itself, the United States had to go hat-in-hand to Japan for certain other critical components. The Japanese Foreign Ministry cooperated, even while warning the United States that there remained

a "strong strain of pacifism in Japanese society."³⁹ In
fact, Japan today has an armed forces, called *self-de-
fense forces*, of about 150,000.

Germany today not only has a thriving industrial
base but an armed forces of almost four hundred
thousand, a "crisis reaction force" of fifty thousand
soldiers, and its troops have participated in U.N. peacekeeping operations in Cambodia and Somalia.⁴⁰ Regarding the U.N., analyst Christopher Story says, "Germany can be relied upon in the future to vote with
Russia" because Germany has "open and secret bilat-
eral treaty obligations towards Moscow."⁴¹

In effect, the United States has been looted of
much of its wealth. The Germans and the Japanese
apparently see the U.N. as useful in this regard by
forcing the deindustrialization of the United States.
One might think that U.N.-sponsored international
regulations restricting industrial development and
economic growth would affect all nations equally. But,
this ignores the fact that Germany and Japan are the
world leaders in so-called environmental technology.
This is made abundantly clear by the book, *Green
Gold*, whose coauthor, Curtis Moore, quotes one Japanese official as saying that "the potential profits" from
such technology "are limitless"—in the "trillions" of
dollars.⁴²

Despite claims by Rush Limbaugh and others that
America is *not* on the decline economically, the facts
are shocking: of the seven major industrialized countries, the United States in 1994 ranked last in national
savings. Japan and Germany were number one and
two. The United States was second to the last in spending on civilian research and development and last in
long-term real growth in the standard of living.⁴³

In the face of these ominous developments showing the United States losing out to Japan and Ger-

many, there is a real need for information and education during this fiftieth anniversary of the U.N.–how the organization has come to be a direct threat to American interests and a tool of foreign governments. Yet, U.N. proponents are targeting children of all ages with pro-U.N. propaganda. A set of taxpayer-funded "National Standards" for teaching U.S. history in the U.S. public schools, grades 5–12, had the effect of whitewashing the world body. The standards, which are said to be undergoing revision, present the United Nations, organized in part by Soviet spy Alger Hiss, as a worthwhile "international peacekeeping organization." Students were instructed to examine where and how the U.N. has promoted peace in the world, not whether the United States should belong to it or not.

There is, in fact, a lot of lingering public sympathy for the United Nations, whose name alone carries some appeal. After all, many people feel uncomfortable over the religious, racial, ethnic, and political differences which characterize many human undertakings and which seem to underpin wars and civil strife. Pro-U.N. activities build off the feeling that if we can't eliminate these differences, perhaps we can transcend them through an organization that emphasizes our common features and searches for ways to work together. Perhaps, they say, this can even work in the military field.

Pressure for world government has been building on the liberal-left side of the political spectrum, especially within the Democratic party, for decades. *Humanist Manifesto II*, a document issued in the early 1970s and signed by such prominent left-wing figures as feminist Betty Friedan, former U.N. official Julian Huxley, and representatives of Americans United for Separation of Church and State, Planned Parenthood and abortion rights organizations, declared:

We deplore the division of humankind on nationalistic grounds. We have reached a turning point in human history where the best option is to transcend the limits of national sovereignty and to move toward the building of a world community in which all sectors of the human family can participate. Thus we look to the development of a system of world law and a world order based upon transnational federal government.[44]

Needless to say, the phrase "transnational federal government" cannot be found in the U.S. Constitution or the Declaration of Independence. These documents, which our elected leaders swear to uphold, do not authorize U.S. involvement in any organization that threatens U.S. sovereignty. Indeed, the Declaration of Independence was itself designed to affirm the independence of the American nation. The only higher authority recognized by this document was God.

Similarly, the U.S. Constitution was designed to affirm the sovereignty of the American state, to place responsibility for decisions affecting the course of the nation on three co-equal branches of government, ultimately accountable to the American people themselves, not to foreign principalities or powers.

Regarding the office of president, with the constitutional responsibilities of commander in chief, the Constitution was quite clear: it had to be held by a natural born citizen. This stipulation was not unimportant. Basically, it affirmed that the United States was going to define its own membership, and out of these members would come its highest office holder. It was an attempt to emphasize that the status of being born in the United States meant something, and that this was critical enough to be a qualification for the highest office in the land. It means that President

Clinton, for all his faults, is commander in chief, not anyone at the U.N.

The key problem is that Clinton and other American elected officials have not defended our nation against its foreign and domestic enemies. And, sad to say, there are people in America today who feel ashamed at being Americans or who feel that it is old-fashioned to act patriotic.

This syndrome, almost like a disease, is an old one. In his classic work, *Suicide of the West*, James Burnham discussed liberals who act patriotic to win votes and those who find flag-waving positively distasteful:

> Liberals, unless they are professional politicians needing votes in the hinterland, are not subject to strong feelings of national patriotism and are likely to feel uneasy at patriotic ceremonies. These, like the organizations in whose conduct they are still manifest, are dismissed by liberals rather scornfully as "flag-waving" and "100 percent Americanism." The national anthem is not customarily sung or the flag shown, unless prescribed by law, at meetings of liberal associations. . . . The purer liberals of the Norman Cousins strain, in the tradition of Eleanor Roosevelt, are more likely to celebrate U.N. Day than the Fourth of July.[45]

The references to Cousins and Roosevelt are significant. Cousins, the former editor of *Saturday Review*, became president of the World Federalist Association. President Clinton praised him, saying, "Norman Cousins worked for world peace and world government." Clinton's sympathetic words, in a letter on White House stationery, were delivered to the World Federalist Association on the occasion of the awarding of its Global Governance Award.[46]

Eleanor Roosevelt, the wife of Franklin Roosevelt, served as a delegate to the U.N. and led a U.N. citizens auxiliary force that later evolved into the United Nations Association of the U.S. (UNA-USA), the premier pro-U.N. lobbying group in America. The UNA-USA today claims 175 community-based chapters, a 135-member Council of Organizations, and operations in New York and Washington, D.C. The UNA-USA says it is now "creating a powerful national constituency for an even better U.N."

Some of the 135-member groups include the American Association of Retired Persons, the AFL-CIO, the American Federation of Teachers, the American Humanist Association, the Anti-Defamation League of B'nai B'rith, the Fund for Peace, the NAACP, the National Education Association, the National Council of Churches, Planned Parenthood Federation of America, the Salvation Army, the Sierra Club, the U.S. Catholic Conference, and the World Federalist Association.

The UNA-USA relies on big foundations for support. In 1991, for example, the Rockefeller Brothers Fund reported a total contribution to the group of $150,000. In 1993, the Rockefeller Brothers Fund provided $90,000.

But, the Ford Foundation appears to be the biggest booster. It reported a grant to the UNA-USA in 1990 of $1,225,000. In 1993, the Ford Foundation reported a grant of $310,000 to the U.N. itself and $250,000 to the U.N. Educational, Scientific and Cultural Organization (UNESCO). "The foundation supports efforts to reinforce the principles governing international relations and to strengthen institutions necessary for cooperative international action," its 1993 annual report says. Toward that end, the foundation copublished *Renewing the United Nations System*, by two former U.N. officials. The Ford Foundation was also a key backer of the 1994 U.N. population conference in Cairo. In 1993, the foundation provided $21,318,637 in funds in the area of "reproductive health and population."

The decision to plow large amounts of tax-exempt foundation money into pro-U.N. activities helps illustrate the fact that a group like the UNA-USA could probably not exist for long on small contributions from ordinary Americans. There is simply no organized grassroots support for the U.N.

The reason is simple: most Americans instinctively know that, despite their sympathy for the concept of "United Nations," the body itself has been a failure, disappointment, and even an enemy of American interests.

In the beginning, author James Burnham argued the U.N. could have served a useful purpose if U.S. administrations had used it to promote American interests:

> At the end of the [World] war, the United States was not only the unquestioned leader of the West, but the most powerful force in the world. By virtue of the Eisenhower army still in being, the nuclear monopoly, and a colossal industrial plant not merely untouched but immensely stimulated by the fighting, the United States was in fact immensely more powerful than any other nation or grouping of nations. . . . What was to be done with this power?

> Abstractly considered, the full creative response to the challenge then presented would have been to establish a Pax Americana on a world scale. This would have meant a guarantee, backed by the power of the United States acting as the integral leader of Western civilization, of a viable world polity: the key to which

would have been the enforcement of nuclear
monopoly and the prohibition of major wars.
Such an arrangement might have been worked
out in any of several forms, some more palat-
able than others; as one variant, it could have
been handled through the United Nations
machinery.[47]

Eventually, however, the Communist and Third
World nations began dominating the world body.
Veteran diplomat Vernon Walters recounts in his book,
Silent Missions, that French President Charles de Gaulle
had warned President Dwight Eisenhower about such
a development during a meeting they had on 3 September 1959. Walters, who attended the meeting, said
that:

> General de Gaulle went on to say that the
> United States was making a great fetish out of
> the United Nations because we controlled a
> majority in that body. But he said that with the
> "flowering of independence," which the United
> States was sponsoring, we would gradually lose
> control of the United Nations to the third world
> nations, which included and would include in
> the future many small states or city-states of a
> few hundred thousand population. The day
> would come when these third world nations in
> control of the United Nations would order the
> United States to do something contrary to its
> fundamental interests, and the United States
> would have made such a golden calf of the
> United Nations that they would have no alter-
> native but to obey what the United Nations
> told them.[48]

Former Republican presidential candidate and
senator Barry Goldwater remembered that approval
by the U.S. Senate of the U.N. Charter was

based largely upon the representations made
by . . . the State Department that it in no sense
constituted a form of World Government and
that neither the Senate nor the American
people need be concerned that the United
Nations or any of its agencies would interfere
with the sovereignty of the United States or
with the domestic affairs of the American
people.[49]

Yet, the U.N. does try to dictate American policy.
Late in 1994, for example, the U.N. deliberately
thumbed its nose at the United States by bringing up,
once again, the issue of the U.S. embargo on trade
and aid to Communist Cuba. Turning its back on our
vital security interests, the U.N. voted 101 to 2 for a
resolution calling on the United States to lift the embargo. The only two countries voting against the resolution were the United States and Israel. Forty-eight
nations abstained. The previous year, *only* eighty-eight
nations had called for an end to the trade ban.

If we followed the U.N.'s advice, of course, important financial relief would flow to the regime of Fidel
Castro and keep Castro himself in power. The embargo is designed to punish a Communist regime which
has been a threat to U.S. security for decades by ex-
porting terrorism and subversion to neighboring countries. Moreover, Cuba hosted Soviet nuclear missiles
targeted at the United States and, according to the
book, *Khrushchev Remembers*, Castro himself asked
Soviet dictator Nikita Khrushchev to launch a preemp-
tive nuclear strike against the United States.[50] Of course,
there is also evidence that Marxist Lee Harvey Oswald,
the assassin of President Kennedy, had links to Cuba
and the Soviet Union.

In another direct attack on our shores, Castro has
unleashed waves of illegal immigrants against America.
Many have gone on to become patriotic Americans

dedicated to overthrowing Castro. But, what is not so widely known is that Castro may have deliberately spread AIDS to the United States through some of them. As many as twenty thousand of the Cubans who were part of the 1980 Mariel boatlift to the United States were homosexual men. Researchers at the University of Miami subsequently confirmed that some of them were infected with AIDS before they entered the United States.[51] Journalist John Crewdson reported,

> The fact that HIV [the virus that is a cause of or co-factor in AIDS] was present in Cuba at least as early as 1980 raises new questions about when and how AIDS arrived in the U.S. and how it was transmitted so rapidly through the homosexual population. Equally intriguing is how HIV found its way to a closed society like Cuba at a time when it was barely present in the U.S.[52]

One theory, Crewdson said, was that Cuban soldiers sent to Angola in the late 1970s brought it back. Another theory is that the disease resulted from Castro's development of chemical and biological weapons. Cuban possession of such weapons was documented in the book *America the Vulnerable*, by Joseph D. Douglass, Jr., and Neil C. Livingstone.[53]

Typically, Castro has accused the CIA of spreading exotic diseases in Cuba and even creating AIDS. In retrospect, such a claim may have been cover for Cuban activities in this area. For whatever reason, it is certainly significant that, by 1988, only 174 Cubans had been reported testing positive for HIV. In Russia, by 1994, only 697 HIV cases had been reported. By contrast, AIDS has claimed more than 200,000 lives in the United States, almost 70 percent of them homosexuals, bisexuals, or intravenous drug users. Castro, too, has been involved in narcotics trafficking into the United States.

Should we be concerned about U.N. resolutions on Cuba that go against our interests? They are certainly relevant as long as the United States pays about one-third of U.N. operating costs. And, Americans are entitled to take offense on the basic grounds that these anti-American plots are being hatched on U.S. territory at U.N. headquarters in New York and amount to blatant interference in U.S. domestic affairs.

However, it is sometimes tempting to dismiss the significance and importance of what the U.N. says and does. The late Murray Rothbard pointed out:

> Most people exhibit a healthy lack of interest in the United Nations and its endless round of activities and conferences, considering them as boring busywork to sustain increasing hordes of tax-exempt bureaucrats, consultants and pundits. All that is true. But there is danger in underestimating the malice of U.N. activities. For underlying all the tedious nonsense is a continuing and permanent drive for international government despotism to be exercised by faceless and arrogant bureaucrats accountable to no one.[54]

Rothbard was referring to the 1994 U.N. Conference on Population and Development, an event featuring a worldwide effort by the Clinton administration and the international population control movement to make abortion a government-guaranteed right. But he could just as well have been referring to the 1992 U.N. Earth Summit, the March 1995 World Summit for Social Development, the Fourth World Conference on Women, or any number of other U.N. conferences or summits.

The essential point made by Rothbard is that "international government despotism" is just as much of a threat as despotism by the U.S. government. In fact, it is more insidious and dangerous because it seems to be further beyond the ability of most Americans to do anything about. After all, the American people have a hard enough time holding their own government accountable.

The hard fact is that we ignore the U.N. at our own peril. U.N. activities, including conferences and resolutions, do affect events in the United States. In a real sense, the U.N. operates as another liberal lobby, capable of manipulating American society on a grand scale. The American political Left realizes it has this weapon even if advocates of the U.N. don't want to acknowledge it. These conferences, for example, sometimes produce treaties that are supposed to be ratified by the various countries. If the U.S. Senate fails to act on such measures, American leftists and their collaborators in Congress and the White House argue that the United States is "out-of-step" with the international community.

Similarly, leftist groups provide important cover for U.S. government initiatives that favor the expansion of U.N. power. For example, the Clinton administration has pursued a deliberate policy of cutting back the size of the U.S. Armed Forces while building up the military operations of the U.N. In fact, Clinton has illegally raided the Pentagon budget to the tune of billions of dollars, depriving our own forces of military readiness funds, to pay for U.N. peacekeeping operations. But, the Institute for Policy Studies (IPS), a group influential in the left wing of the Democratic party, argues that the Clinton administration hasn't gone far enough. The IPS says, "It's time to pare down this bloated [Pentagon] bureaucracy to post-Cold War realities, and place more of the burden of preventing war on the United Nations." Toward this end, the IPS announced that its cofounder Richard Barnet, "along with a group of retired generals and political activists at the Massachusetts Institute of

Technology (MIT)," were preparing a study making
the case for the United States to support "stronger,
better funded U.N. peacekeeping."[55]

Despite what Senator Goldwater thought the U.S.
Senate was promised when it ratified the U.N. charter,
the U.N. has been caught blatantly interfering in U.S.
domestic politics. The clandestine role played by U.N.
bureaucrats in the notorious big government health
care scheme that the Clinton administration tried to
ram through the U.S. Congress in 1994 is one example. This untold story has been detailed in George
Grant's book, *The Family Under Siege*, in which the
U.N.-affiliated World Health Organization (WHO) is
named as a major player in the scheme. Grant dis-
closes that the WHO laid the groundwork for the plan
years ago by preparing various materials, claiming there
was a "health-care crisis" in the United States that
could only be solved by government intervention on
a massive scale. These materials were distributed at a
national health-care forum sponsored by the WHO
and the U.S. federal Department of Health and Human Services. Interestingly, Grant says, the participants were told during one session to act as a "health-
care alliance resource delegation committee," making
decisions on who should get health care. Of course,
the phrase "health-care alliance" is strikingly similar to
the "health alliances" in the Clinton plan. This isn't
surprising because Grant reports that the WHO "lent
its full resources to Hillary Clinton's secretive task
force to draft the initial health-care reform package
for the U.S."[56]

The U.N.'s involvement in the Clinton health plan
is instructive. It demonstrates that when the U.S. government moves toward bigger government which can
serve U.N. interests, the U.N. plays an active supporting role. What this means, in practice, is that the U.N.,
created under the auspices of a Democratic adminis-

tration, has become a key ally of subsequent Democratic administrations that want to expand the power and reach of the federal government.

In fact, one U.N. agency made no secret of its pleasure that the Clinton administration had taken power in the United States in 1992. The U.N. Children's Fund (UNICEF), often called one of the most admired U.N. agencies, declared in its 1994 report on "The State of the World's Children" that "many of the policy objectives of the Clinton administration . . . point to a new deal for American children." It went on to praise "universal health coverage," a reference to the Clinton health care scheme, as well as passage of the Family and Medical Leave Act, which was "blocked and weakened by the past two Administrations." The report didn't mention that Republican administrations had objected to the measure on the grounds that it constituted unwarranted and unnecessary government interference in the affairs of American businesses.

Incredibly, the document went on to spew some dangerous disinformation regarding the nature of America's failed welfare system and what must be done to reform it. The UNICEF report declared that, "Some of the changes affecting American children—such as the sharp rise in single parenthood—are beyond the immediate reach of government."[57] This was a blatant falsehood, of course, because the federal government has been rewarding single parenthood by providing more money for women having children out of wedlock, decimating families, and leaving many young children fatherless. As we will see, however, the U.N.'s answer to this problem may well be *more* government, in the form of official distribution of condoms, contraceptives, and "safe-sex" brochures.

In any case, it was extremely significant that the UNICEF report was full of praise for Marian Wright

Edelman, head of the Children's Defense Fund (CDF) and a staunch opponent of dismantling the liberal welfare state. The CDF, previously chaired by Hillary Rodham Clinton, has lobbied for Senate ratification of the proposed U.N. Convention on the Rights of the Child, a treaty that affirms children's rights against their parents and advocates more government involvement in decisions affecting the family.[58] In Britain, where the treaty was ratified, the U.N. conducted an "international audit" of the country's compliance with the document and issued a report warning government officials to eliminate such practices as permitting private schools to spank students.[59]

Typically, the U.N. pays lips service to the idea that nations retain their sovereignty when they get involved in U.N. activities. However, the reality is that when the United States moves in the direction of reasserting American independence, even control over our own borders, the U.N. plays an obstructionist role. An example of this trend lies in the hostile reaction of U.N. bureaucrats and their U.S. allies to passage of California's Proposition 187 in 1994, a measure designed to cut off welfare to illegal immigrants.

Even before Proposition 187 passed by an overwhelming 59 to 41 percent margin, Alfredo Witschi, a regional representative of the United Nations High Commissioner for Refugees, was expressing the fear that the measure would have "alarming consequences" for illegal immigrants. After passage, liberal-left activists called upon the U.N. to intervene in California's affairs on the grounds that Proposition 187 would violate "international human rights." Some activists even urged the U.N. to send "human rights monitors" to the state. Delores Wardell, vice president of the Orange County, California, chapter of the United Nations Association, condemned the measure in strident terms, saying:

> In this era of hate crimes, Proposition 187,
> homophobia, xenophobia and extremism, there
> needs to be a movement devoted to under-
> standing, compassion and tolerance.[60]

Another example of the U.N. interfering in the domestic affairs of the United States occurred in 1995 when the U.N. Human Rights Commission held hearings to review charges that America was racist and holding "political prisoners," such as Puerto Rican activists imprisoned for criminal acts. Unfortunately, the United States had invited the scrutiny by ratifying the International Covenant on Civil and Political Rights, a measure that required the U.S. government to issue a report on the state of human rights in America and which opened the door for leftist groups to hold the United States up to their standards of political correctness. Such meddling in American affairs would be laughable were it not for the fact that left-wing activists see it as an opportunity to mock and humiliate the United States.

These hearings resulted in a U.N. report criticizing the U.S. human rights record and the convening of a tribunal where American officials had to appear to answer the charges. Among other things, U.N. bureaucrats wanted to know why the United States had not adopted the Equal Rights Amendment, why Proposition 187 was allowed to pass, and whether the United States was applying capital punishment in a racially fair manner.

In order to put an end to such meddling in our internal affairs and to stop the emerging world government, it is necessary to draw upon the patriotism of the American people. One poll found that 93 percent of Americans surveyed said they have emotional feelings when they hear the national anthem, with more than 30 percent describing their feelings as "ex-

tremely emotional."[61] These expressions of nationalism and pride stem from a sense of what America
represents and what it is supposed to stand for in the
world. Part of it lies in the recognition that many have
sacrificed their lives and limbs to keep America free
and independent. There is also a belief by many that
America was divinely inspired, and that God guides
our destiny even today.

The national anthem is just one expression of
American patriotism. The Pledge of Allegiance to the
Flag, which is still allowed in the public schools (despite its reference to "One Nation Under God"), is
another. And, the flag itself is something that Americans treasure and want protected. By March of 1995,
forty-six of the American states had passed memorial-
izing resolutions supporting a constitutional amendment to protect the U.S. flag from physical desecration. The Citizens Flag Alliance, a coalition of more
than eighty national patriotic organizations led by the
American Legion, is working intensely to get a flag-
protection constitutional amendment through Congress and the states. All of this is in response to a 1989
Supreme Court decision allowing flag desecration
under the First Amendment.

If this patriotism is channelled into a massive campaign to save American sovereignty, there is hope for
America. But, time is running out.

Notes

1. Leslie H. Gelb, "Quelling the Teacup Wars," *Foreign Affairs* (November/December 1994): 6.

2. *Human Development Report 1994* (New York: Oxford University Press, 1994): 70.

3. Ruben Mendez, "Harnessing the Global Currency Market for the Global Common Good," *Choices* (April 1995): 16–17.

4. "Helms Weighs in Against WTO," *Human Events* (25 November 1994): 4.

5. Richard N. Gardner, "The Hard Road to World Order," *Foreign Affairs* (April 1974): 556–576.

6. Ibid., 563.

7. See Cliff Kincaid, "NAFTA Will Encourage Illegal Drug Trafficking," *Human Events* (11 September 1993): 5.

8. American Coalition for Competitive Trade, Inc., news release, April 1995.

9. "Drugs: A Global Crisis," *World Goodwill Newsletter* (1994): no. 4, 3,4.

10. "Listening to Elders," *USA Weekend* (3-5 June 1994): 5, 6.

11. Stephanie Haynes, letter to Ms. Sylvie A. Bryant, UNDCP, 10 August 1994.

12. See William A. Donohue, *The Politics of the American Civil Liberties Union* (New Brunswick: Transaction Books, 1985), 281.

13. "European Parliament Commission Favors Legalization of Cannabis," National Organization for the Reform of Marijuana Laws release, 2 February 1995.

14. Statement by the Honorable Conrad K. Harper, legal adviser, United States Department of State, Agenda Item 137: Report of the International Law Commission on the World of its Forty-Sixth Session, International Criminal Court, United Nations General Assembly, 49th Session, Sixth Committee, U.S. Mission to the United Nations, Press Release, 25 October 1994.

15. *Drug Policy Report*, March 1995, 12.

16. "HHS Releases High School Drug Abuse and 'Dawn' Surveys," Department of Health and Human Services, 12 December 1994.

17. Edwin Feulner, "Those Roaring '80s and the Greed Screed," *Washington Times* (14 August 1995), 134.

18. "Drug Policy Reform Gets Boost," news release, the Drug Policy Foundation, 11 July 1994.

19. *Drug Policy Report*, vol. 1, no. 11, December 1994.

20. "Banks Accused of Drug Money Laundering," Inter Press Service, 22 August 1990.

21. Reuter, "Soros Takes Colombian Bank Stake," *Financial Times* (20 August 1994): 11. Michael Scott, "Colombia: Galinskis to Expand Banco de Colombia Abroad," Reuter News Service (29 January 1994): 11.

22. George Soros, Address to Committee to Protect Journalists, 9 November 1994.

23. Cliff Kincaid, "Is There A Comeuppance in Ted's Future," *Washington Times* (20 August 1987).

24. Cliff Kincaid, "Ted Turner's Pro-Abortion Politics," *Wanderer* (11 September 1986).

25. See UN50 Global Programme, Fiftieth Anniversary Secretariat, United Nations.

26. "The Spirit of Goodwill," *World Goodwill Newsletter* (1994): n.p. 3., 3.

27. UN50 Global Programme, Fiftieth Anniversary Secretariat.

28. Alvin Toffler, *The Third Wave* (New York: William Morrow and Company, Inc., 1980), 340.

29. Terence Roth, *Wall Street Journal* (23 January 1995): A13B, as quoted in the Howard Phillips Issues and Strategy Bulletin, 28 February 1995.

30. Victor Smart, "Clinton Backs United States of Europe," *European* (24-30 March 1995): 1.

31. Christopher Story, ed. and pub., *International Currency Review*, vol. 22, no. 3-4 (London: World Reports Limited, 1994).

32. Toffler, *The Third Wave*, 448.

33. Alvin and Heidi Toffler, *Creating a New Civilization: The Politics of the Third Wave* (Washington, D.C.: The Progress and Freedom Foundation, 1994), 15,16.

34. Ibid., 57.

35. Michael G. Zey, *Seizing the Future* (New York: Simon & Schuster, 1994), 27, and author's interview with Michael Zey, January 1995.

36. "EU Backs Japan Seat," *Washington Times* (11 March 1995): 7.

37. Ibid., American Coalition for Competitive Trade.

38. Martin and Susan Tolchin, *Selling Our Security* (Alfred A. Knopf: New York, 1992), 171.

39. Ibid., 172.

40. John Marks, "Germany Conquers the Cringe Factor," *U.S. News & World Report* (20 March 1995): 50, 51.

41. Christopher Story, "Soviet/Russian 'Peacekeeping,' Haiti and Georgia," *Soviet Analyst*, vol. 23, no. 1.

42. Curtis A. Moore, letter to "Fellow Member" of Society of Environmental Journalists, undated.

43. "Competitiveness Index," Council on Competitiveness, 1994.

44. *Humanist Manifestos I and II* (New York: Prometheus Books, 1973), 21, 27-31.

45. James Burnham, *Suicide of the West* (New York: Arlington House, 1964), 84-85.

46. Dennis Laurence Cuddy, Ph.D., "Secret Records Revealed," (The Plymouth Rock Foundation: Marlborough, New Hampshire, 1995).

47. Ibid., 259.

48. Vernon A. Walters, *Silent Missions* (New York: Doubleday & Company, Inc. 1978), 491.

49. Barry Goldwater, *Why Not Victory?* (New York: McGraw-Hill Book Company Inc., 1962), 103.

50. Jerrold L. Schecter with Vyacheslav V. Luchkov, *Krushchev Remembers* (Little, Brown and Company: Boston, 1990).

51. John Crewdson, "Cuba Link Sought in Spread of AIDS," *Chicago Tribune* (31 January 1988): 6.

52. Ibid.

53. Joseph D. Douglass, Jr., and Neil C. Livingstone, *America the Vulnerable* (D.C. Heath and Company, 1987), 151, 152.

54. Murray N. Rothbard, "Population Control," *Free Market* (November 1994): 4.

55. "Dear Friend," *IPS Mailing* (30 November 1994): 2.

56. George Grant, *The Family Under Siege* (Minnesota: Bethany House Publishers, 1994), 209.

57. *The State of the World's Children 1994*, UNICEF (New York: Oxford University Press, 1994), 46, 47.

58. Phyllis Schlafly, "Havoc Lurking in Children's Treaty," *Washington Times* (27 December 1992).

59. Mike Farris, president, Home School Legal Defense Association, "Update on U.N. Convention on the Rights of the Child," newsletter, 13 February 1995.

60. Delores Wardell and Suzanne Darweesh, "Commentary on Society," *Los Angeles Times*, Orange County edition (2 October 1994): part B, 7.

61. "Cultural Conservatism," *American Enterprise* (November–December 1994): The American Enterprise Institute.

The U.N.

The World Army

President Clinton, despite his constitutional position as commander in chief, has engineered a direct assault on the command and control of our troops. Acting without any constitutional authority or even congressional authorization, he has turned over our troops to a group of bureaucrats, many of them foreigners, at the U.N. Once the American people get a clear understanding of what has happened to the soldiers, sailors, airmen, and marines that they so cherish, they will be prepared to march on the White House and the Capitol.

Three years ago, according to American major Joseph F. Napoli, the U.N. Department of Peacekeeping Operations had a staff of twenty-three with only six military officers. Under Clinton, it has grown to a staff of 350 with 116 military officers from thirty-five countries.[1] Major Napoli should know; he is the executive officer to the military adviser to U.N. Secretary General Boutros Boutros-Ghali.

Americans should pause for a moment and consider what is happening.

Traditionally, being an American has meant having American interests protected and defended by the

Armed Forces of the United States. U.S. military forces
have always been viewed as a symbol of national pride
and national sovereignty. The concept of having a
military implies there is a government that will act to
protect the American nation-state and not sacrifice
the sovereign rights that grew out of the Declaration
of Independence and the U.S. Constitution.

On another level, the idea of being an American
means voting for a government that represents American interests. At the top of this government is the
president—the commander in chief—and the Congress,
given the constitutional powers to regulate the Armed
Forces of the U.S. The intention of the founding fathers was to have American political leaders follow the
Constitution and represent the American people, not
foreign or alien interests.

However, some popular "futurists" have attempted
to condition people into believing that it is inevitable
and worthwhile that elements of a world government,
such as a world army, are taking shape. They frame
these developments in the best possible light. For
example, John Naisbitt, author of the best seller
Megatrends, says the emergence of U.N. peacekeeping
forces is a positive move because they can stamp out
human rights violations around the world. In his book,
Global Paradox, he wrote that:

> The good news is that human-rights violations
> are being exposed whenever they occur, and
> the international community, not any single
> country, is assuming the role of enforcer and
> peacekeeper.[2]

Naisbitt's comments are extremely revealing. He
seems to be saying that the international community
has come to the conclusion that the U.S. military alone
can't be trusted to keep the peace. This is a critical
point. The United Nations has expanded its role in

peacekeeping activities dramatically over the last two years while President Clinton has made drastic reductions in spending on our own national defense. This is no accident.

The official figures are startling. In 1992, the U.N. had peacekeeping operations in eleven countries, with 11,496 personnel deployed in them. By 1994, that had dramatically risen to peacekeeping activities in seventeen countries, with 73,393 personnel involved. The U.N. budget for peacekeeping alone had risen during the same period from $1.7 billion to $3.6 billion, of which the United States was assessed about $1.2 billion.[3]

But, these official figures may greatly understate the cost of U.N. peacekeeping operations. Sen. Bob Dole, a leading critic of the U.N., has cited figures from the General Accounting Office showing that U.N. peacekeeping cost the United States more than $10 billion from fiscal year 1992 to fiscal year 1995.[4] The difference could be ascribed to how much the United States was assessed versus how much the Clinton administration actually spent. In other words, the administration was spending money it didn't have, a practice that Dole noted is illegal in other government programs. Dole had proposed that the U.S. contribution to the U.N. be limited to the amount appropriated by Congress. Incredibly, however, this common-sense proposal was denounced as a threat to the constitutional powers of the president by the Clinton administration!

In any case, as Naisbitt suggests, the U.N. has grown far beyond being a simple forum for debate. It is acting, in essence, like a world government, with a world army that will, if trends continue, perhaps rival the United States as a superpower. It is not beyond the realm of possibility that such a force, comprised of German or Japanese troops, could be deployed on

U.S. soil. But, the ominous development, from the
U.S. perspective, is that the world army already includes U.S. soldiers as its front line troops. And, the
realistic possibility has to be entertained that these
troops could one day be deployed against American
citizens.

Even the official figures show that the creation of
this world army has been accomplished largely since
the advent of the Clinton administration. This should
not have come as any great surprise because the essence of the policy had been laid out in advance in
Mandate for Change, the book expressing the views of
the Democratic Leadership Council (DLC) and its think
tank, the Progressive Policy Institute. Chairmen of the
DLC have included President Clinton, Senators Sam
Nunn and Charles Robb, and Congressman Richard
Gephardt. Vice President Al Gore was a DLC member
when he was in the U.S. Senate.

DLC members have called themselves "new Democrats" and the organization has cultivated an image as
a "moderate conservative" group. However, like the
far Left Institute for Policy Studies, which wants to
expand the power and scope of the U.N., the "moderate" DLC presented a foreign policy that put heavy
emphasis on the U.N. In a chapter entitled "U.S. Global Leadership for Democracy," Will Marshall urged
the new administration to provide "vigorous U.S. support" for U.N. conferences and endorsed more U.S.
involvement in U.N. military operations, saying:

> The U.S. should support the creation of a
> United Nations rapid-deployment force that
> could take on policing and relief duties that
> might otherwise fall into our lap by
> default. . . . This would not require the U.N. to
> maintain a large standing army, but rather a
> force that could be called up from units of

national armed forces—including our own—and earmarked and trained in advance.[5]

It's apparent that Marshall wanted to avoid embracing the controversial concept of a "large standing army" for the U.N. But, his "rapid deployment force," comprised of well-trained "units of national armed forces" that could be called up at any time, amounts to the same thing. The clear intention has been to create an environment under which American forces can be placed under U.N. command and control on a regular basis.

In order to create the circumstances under which this policy could be implemented, apologists for the administration have peddled the notion that this was really nothing new, and that Americans have served under foreign commanders in the past, including U.N. commanders. But, today's circumstances are radically different. The critical difference is that the Clinton administration has clearly coordinated its efforts with U.N. plans to activate Article 43 of the U.N. Charter, which authorizes a standing U.N. force.

It is impossible to understand the Clinton administration's deliberate actions without taking into account what U.N. Secretary General Boutros-Ghali had openly proclaimed in his "Agenda for Peace" report of 31 January 1992. He explained:

> Under Article 42 of the [U.N.] Charter, the Security Council has the authority to take military action to maintain or restore international peace and security. While such action should only be taken when all peaceful means have failed, the option of taking it is essential to the credibility of the United Nations as a guarantor of international security. This will require bringing into being, through negotiations, the special agreements foreseen in Article 43 of

the Charter, whereby Member States under-
take to make armed forces, assistance and facilities available to the Security Council for the
purposes stated in Article 42, not only on an
ad hoc basis but on a permanent basis.[6]

There can be no serious doubt that the Clinton
administration came into office determined to implement Boutros-Ghali's plan. President Clinton put into
office a number of people who were already committed to expanding U.N. power at the expense of the
United States.

One of these key people was Strobe Talbott, the
former *Time* magazine journalist and very close friend
of the president's, who served as ambassador-at-large
to the former Soviet Union before becoming deputy
secretary of state. He was confirmed to his post despite the fact that his views in favor of world government were already out in the open. He had written an
article in *Time* magazine under the headline, "The
Birth of the Global Nation," forecasting that in the
next century "nationhood as we know it will be obso-
lete" and that "all states will recognize a single, global
authority." Talbott added, "A phrase briefly fashion-
able in the mid-20th century—'citizen of the world'—
will have assumed real meaning by the end of the
21st." Talbott went on to say that it had taken the
events in "our own wondrous and terrible century to
clinch the case for world government."[7]

President Clinton's selection of Gen. John M.
Shalikashvili, the NATO commander, to succeed Gen.
Colin Powell as chairman of the U.S. Joint Chiefs of
Staff, also raised concern in some quarters. Journalist
Fred Barnes had reported that General Shalikashvili
had endorsed the expansion of the U.N. in military
affairs, with NATO playing an auxiliary role. The gen-
eral was quoted as saying, "NATO should not be viewed

as a tool of the United Nations, but rather as a partner where the United Nations establishes the moral and legal mandate for specific action and the alliance (NATO) provides the tools, or at least the majority of the tools, to fulfill that mandate."[8]

Another significant development was President Clinton's appointment of radical left-wing activist and ACLU attorney Morton Halperin to a new post in the Department of Defense as assistant secretary of defense for democracy and peacekeeping. Halperin's pro-U.N. views were also a matter of public record, having written that:

> The United States should explicitly surrender the right to intervene unilaterally in the internal affairs of other countries by overt military means or by covert operations. Such self-restraint would bar interventions like those in Grenada or Panama unless the United States first gained the explicit consent of the international community acting through the [U.N.] Security Council or a regional organization.[9]

Halperin was nominated for the post at a time when former U.S. Ambassador to the U.N. Jeane Kirkpatrick was saying that Clinton's foreign policy was already amounting to "doing what the U.N. calls on us to do."[10] Ironically, Halperin's pro-U.N. views proved to be some of the least controversial that he held. Much of the criticism of his nomination focused on his support of Philip Agee, the defector from the CIA with close ties to Communist Cuba.

In the end, the U.S. Senate failed to confirm Halperin to his post. However, President Clinton was so determined to have him playing a central role in his administration that he named him to a staff position on the super-secret National Security Council, a post that didn't require Senate confirmation. Since then, it has been confirmed that Halperin has been trying to convince Clinton to lift the U.S. economic embargo against Cuba and save the Communist regime there. Rep. Robert Menendez, a Democrat, has led calls for Halperin's ouster.

Under Halperin's guiding hand, the Clinton administration rushed into U.N. peacekeeping so fast that officials ignored resolving the critical issue of the fate of those American troops who might be assigned to U.N. operations.

Personal tragedies had already occurred. One involved Marine Col. William R. Higgins, who was transferred to an assignment with the United Nations in July 1987. On 17 February 1988, he disappeared in Lebanon, kidnapped by pro-Iranian terrorists, and later executed. The exact date of death is uncertain, for his death was made known only when his captors released a videotape showing his lifeless body hanging from a rope. Officially, he was declared dead on 6 July 1990. His remains were eventually recovered and interred at Quantico National Cemetery, 30 December 1991. How his body was recovered was especially gruesome. His widow, Lt. Col. Robin Higgins, said the body had decomposed and was dumped on a Beirut street on her birthday.[11]

A critical fact about the Higgins case was that, because he was a member of a U.N. mission, he was not labeled by the U.S. government as a POW or MIA when he disappeared. Instead, he was merely labeled a "hostage." His widow explains what this meant:

> Because Col. Higgins was always a "hostage" and never a "prisoner," there were never any demands of international rules of treatment, no Red Cross visits, no insistence on medical care or humane treatment, and no POW medal. The State Department, not the Defense De-

partment, had the lead. That meant diplomacy, not military might.[12]

She declared this clearly unacceptable, noting that several lessons should be drawn from the case:

> The United Nations cannot protect Americans. Let's not expect them to do so. Even though American service members may wear the blue beret of the U.N., they still wear American uniforms. If killed or taken captive, they will be treated as American servicemen. American men and women in uniform go into harm's way because they believe they are doing something important for their country and that America will come after them when they fall. Let's not fail them.[13]

These lessons, however, were completely ignored by the Clinton administration when it expanded the involvement of U.S. troops in Somalia in 1993 and placed them directly under U.N. command. Clearly, Somalia was meant to be the first real test of the U.N.'s world army concept. In Somalia, U.N. Commanders were going to be directing U.S. and other forces in what would euphemistically be called a "nontraditional mission." If this was successful, the world army could grow in scope and influence.

In a sense, of course, President Clinton had inherited the situation in Somalia. President Bush had originally dispatched U.S. forces to the African country on a humanitarian mission to feed starving people. He had refused to get the U.N. involved in the effort initially, and his intention was to withdraw the troops after the humanitarian effort was over. But, President Clinton decided to transform the mission into a "nation-building" scheme under U.N. control. From the perspective of Clinton and his globalist-minded advisers, it held out the hope of building up the power and prestige of the U.N.

But, the politically correct vision of a multilateral force quickly ran into serious difficulties. On top of all the other problems that confront a military operation, the question was being asked by our own forces: Whose side was the U.N. on?

In one embarrassing incident, U.S. Army Rangers were ordered to raid a building in Mogadishu that contained the offices of the U.N. Development Program in the hopes of apprehending supporters of fugitive warlord Mohammed Farah Aidid. It was believed that Aidid's supporters used the building after hours to plot terrorist attacks. However, the building turned out to be empty. One military official said the terrorists had been there but moved out, after receiving advance word of the impending raid. From whom? U.N. officials were key suspects. *Washington Post* correspondent Keith B. Richburg reported that, "Peacekeeping troops who recently raided an Aidid stronghold were surprised to find among documents there U.N. papers that earlier had been thrown into the garbage at the U.N. headquarters compound in Mogadishu, according to officials."[14]

Aidid, who was being blamed for much of the violence, clearly saw the U.N. as a target of opportunity. Michael Gordon of the *New York Times* said Aidid "saw the transfer of command as an opportunity to engage in a test of wills with the United Nations." Shortly thereafter, the first test came: Aidid's forces ambushed two groups of Pakistani U.N. peacekeepers, killing twenty-three of them. But, it also meant that American troops involved in the effort were going to be singled out for attack.

This "test" came when one hundred elite U.S. infantrymen were deployed in a military operation that was intended to capture Aidid himself. The result was a fifteen-hour battle and a massacre in the streets of Mogadishu. Eighteen U.S. soldiers were immediately killed, another seventy-eight were wounded, two American helicopters were shot down and one pilot captured. It took United Nations forces more than nine hours to reach the U.S. troops, who lacked heavy equipment and had been calling for back-up. The body of one dead U.S. soldier was dragged through the streets by ropes tied to his feet, while another was stripped naked and surrounded by a mob shouting "Victory!"

Media coverage of fallout from the tragic ambush was a severe setback for the advocates of the world army. The massacre illustrated the futility, even insanity, of having the United States rely on the U.N. for backup in military operations. The world army's first major test had backfired, with disastrous consequences for American families and their loved ones. Boys and girls lost fathers, and wives lost husbands because the Clinton administration was determined to use American troops as cannon fodder in an experiment conceived by "Commander" Boutros-Ghali.

It could have been worse. The other misguided aspect of the affair involved treatment by the U.S. government of one of our own soldiers—U.S. Army Chief Warrant Officer Michael Durant, the pilot who was captured alive by Aidid's forces. Like Colonel Higgins before him, Durant was not labeled a POW. Then-Department of Defense (DOD) spokesman Kathleen DeLaski labeled him a mere "detainee," whatever that was. One military official described Durant's status as being "illegally detained as a U.N. person." Rep. Sam Johnson, a POW during the Vietnam War, was livid, saying after Durant's eventual release:

As of right now, Durant has not gotten a POW
medal. If he wasn't a POW, I don't know what
the heck he was. He certainly deserves one.
I'm here to tell you I've got one, and I'll give
mine to him if the DOD can't get theirs out
and do what's right by that guy, because he
certainly deserves it.[15]

The ambush and massacre of U.S. forces led to
the resignation of Defense Secretary Les Aspin, who
took responsibility for the failure to supply our forces
with the heavy equipment they needed to defend themselves. But, the responsibility clearly rested with the
president himself, the nominal commander in chief.
Later, when Clinton met with the families of two soldiers who had been killed attempting to rescue those
forces in Somalia, to give their sons the first Congressional Medals of Honor since the Vietnam War, he
extended his hand to Herbert Shughart, the father of
one of them, who bluntly declared, "The blame for my
son's death rests with the White House and with you.
You are not fit to command."[16]

Ironically, it could be argued that Clinton had
abdicated his role as commander in chief, and that
Boutros-Ghali had been the one truly in charge. In
any case, Clinton still bore responsibility for putting
U.S. troops at the disposal of the world army. Eventually, because of rising public disgust with the entire
Somalia debacle, Clinton ordered a pullout of U.S.
forces, leaving the U.N. to fend for itself. By September of 1994, the *Washington Post* was reporting from
Mogadishu that, "After the deaths of more than 100
U.N. peacekeepers here—including thirty-six Americans—Somalia is as unstable and devoid of hope today
as at any time since it collapsed into anarchy in January 1991. Clan-based Somali factions are rearming rapidly, kidnapping of foreigners is again commonplace,
and U.N. peacekeepers are dying in record numbers."[17]

By early 1995, however, President Clinton had ordered American marines back to Somalia–to rescue the rest of the U.N. troops! But, even the withdrawal was not without incident. The pull-out hit a snag when about fifteen U.N. staff members in Mogadishu were seized and held hostage by thirty armed Somalis, who had been formerly employed by the U.N. in the country and had not been paid. Journalists also predicted a fight between the warring clans over who would control the U.N. compound when it was evacuated, with one reporter saying that, "most U.N. officials and Somali residents fear a battle over the compound will only be the first in a series of fresh conflicts over the valuable assets left behind by U.N. troops."[18]

But, that spectacle would not prove to be as embarrassing as how the U.S. Marines deployed to Somalia to rescue the U.N. forces were equipped–with "non-lethal" weapons such as sticky foam and rubber bullets as their first line of defense. As former Ambassador Kirkpatrick noted, these weapons were mandated by the U.N.'s "strange and unusual" rules of engagement, which do not permit peacekeepers to draw their guns unless their own lives are directly threatened.[19]

In the end, the two-year operation had cost the U.N. over $2 billion, of which the United States had contributed more than $1 billion in men, material, and services. The evacuation alone was estimated to cost about $50 million.[20]

But, the advocates of a world army have always had contingency plans. If it doesn't quite work out in one place, it can be tried somewhere else. They aim to do it "right," regardless of how many American lives are lost and how many families are shattered in the process.

While the situation in Somalia was running out of control, the administration was proceeding with a plan to involve U.S. troops in a bloody civil war in Bosnia. This, too, proved to be a fiasco.

Bosnia was actually a European problem. But Europe, despite its newfound "unity," could not figure out what to do. The Clinton administration began intervening in Bosnia in February 1993 by deploying American air power through NATO against the Bosnian Serbs, the Communist faction backed by Russia. It seemed like a worthy objective, at least on paper, except for the fact that the same problems confronting the U.N. in Somalia became painfully obvious. In this case, however, it was worse; both the U.N. and NATO were involved, complicating the command structure.

Sen. Paul Coverdell noted that when Pentagon spokeswoman Kathleen de Laski was asked to explain who would authorize NATO air strikes on Serb positions, she referred reporters to the United Nations for clarification, saying, "Why don't you call the U.N.? That's what I suggest."[21]

Confusion was rampant. One week before de Laski referred reporters to the U.N., Joint Chiefs Chairman General Shalikashvili was telling the Senate Armed Services Committee that the U.N. could request but not order air strikes by NATO in Bosnia. However, one day later, NATO Secretary Gen. Manfred Woerner said the strikes would have to be ordered "in coordination" with Boutros-Ghali. When asked for clarification, he declined to be specific.

Senator Coverdell attacked the chain of command, saying, "The President must not unilaterally cede U.S. authority to decision makers such as Boutros Boutros-Ghali who have no accountability to the American public. The issue is far too important and the consequences are too grave."[22]

Indeed it was. But, the situation was worse than most people realized. In Bosnia, the initial problem consisted of the fact that the U.N. had declared an international arms embargo against Bosnia, affecting not only the Serbs, who had weapons, but their victims, who needed them. In other words, it was because of the U.N. embargo that the United States and the U.N. felt they had to get further involved in the fighting.

After Europe initially balked at getting involved, troops from Britain, France, and other countries were deployed into Bosnia as U.N. peacekeepers, as a check on Serb aggression. Ironically, however, the presence of these U.N. forces was then used as an argument against lifting the embargo, as proposed by Sen. Bob Dole, because it was feared that weapons shipments to anti-Serb forces would intensify the war and threaten the lives of those same peacekeepers! Then, as in Somalia, a proposed withdrawal of the U.N. forces became a potential problem because of fears that U.N. military equipment would fall into Serb hands.

Thanks to the U.N., the situation had degenerated into lunacy. Appropriately, one of the most humiliating events for the world body occurred when its "military leader," Boutros-Ghali, was snubbed on a peace mission to the area by the leader of the Bosnian Serbs. Author David Rieff commented:

> In six months, we have gone from the spectacle of U.N. officials insisting, in the teeth of all the evidence, that within the framework of its mandate the peacekeeping had been and remained a success, to their racking their brains to figure out how to extricate themselves from the Balkans. Perhaps what changed their minds was the deaths of Bangladeshi peacekeepers in Bihac, the shelling of the Bosnian President's office by the Bosnia Serbs while Yasushi Akashi [the U.N. Special Representative for former Yugoslavia] was inside and the humiliating

spectacle of the U.N. Secretary General himself, Boutros Boutros-Ghali, arriving in Sarajevo
believing he would meet with Radovan Karadzic,
only to have the leader of the Bosnian Serbs
turn down a meeting except at his own headquarters in Pale. Given the U.N.'s record of
self-abasement before the Serbs, it is almost
surprising that Boutros-Ghali did not agree to
this as well.[23]

At the same time this U.N. embarrassment was
unfolding, another potential fiasco was being unveiled
in Haiti, as thousands of U.S. troops were eventually
sent under U.N. auspices on a mission to restore to
power the former Haitian president, Jean Bertrand
Aristide, a Catholic priest kicked out of his Catholic
order for preaching violence. Aristide, an advocate of
Marxist-oriented "liberation theology," had been
evicted as president by military leaders who accused
him of violating the Haitian Constitution.

The intervention in Haiti was significant for many
reasons. In a clear break with the Reagan-Bush policy
of supporting anti-Communist liberation movements,
it represented an unprecedented effort by the Clinton
administration to use American military power with
U.N. backing to install pro-Communist forces in control of a country. In effect, Clinton was intervening on
the losing side of the "Cold War."

But, it was also noteworthy because of U.N. involvement. Analyzing the proposal for U.S. action in
Haiti, the Republican Research Committee declared,

> The U.N. was meant to be an organization of
> national governments meeting to resolve dis-
> putes between nations as an alternative to gen-
> eral warfare. For it to become involved in the
> process of selecting national governments is a
> fundamental enlargement of its mandate. Yet
> this is a process Clinton has sought to encour-

age in accordance with a liberal worldview that imagines the U.N. to be a proto-world government.[24]

Publicly, the administration acted as if the crisis in Haiti were similar to Iraq's invasion of Kuwait—an obvious deception. It sought and received a U.N. Security Council resolution authorizing action in Haiti using the same terminology as that used before U.S. intervention against Iraq. But, the regime in Haiti did not threaten the United States or our neighbors. Also, in contrast to the Persian Gulf action, in which the Bush administration eventually sought and received congressional backing, the Clinton administration showed complete disdain for Congress by simply ignoring the coequal body charged with the constitutional responsibility for declaring war.

The administration saw that Haiti represented an opportunity for both the Clinton presidency and the U.N. to reassert themselves, at the expense of Congress. Internal documents out of the U.N. revealed that Clinton Deputy Secretary of State Strobe Talbott was secretly conferring on an on-going basis with officials of the U.N., including Boutros-Ghali and his special representative to Haiti, Dante Caputo.[25]

One memorandum declared that Haiti was a "test case" for the United States and the U.N. Another document revealed that U.S. officials had shunned a negotiated settlement, with Caputo saying that "the U.S. has acted as a check regarding a diplomatic solution, creating a situation where intervention has become almost inevitable." Further, one memo declared that, "The U.S. Administration believes that an invasion of Haiti is its best option."

It continued:

In the same way, the U.S. President's principal advisors are of the opinion that this option not only constitutes a lesser evil but that it is desirable in political terms. Thus it is felt that the current public opposition to an intervention will change radically once it has come about. The Americans see in this type of action an opportunity to show, after the strong media criticism of the Administration, the President's decision-making ability, his firmness and his leadership in the area of international policy.[26]

U.N. officials, concerned about their own reputations, thought the scheme could backfire against them. One document reported that Caputo believed,

it will all be a disaster because the U.S. will saddle the U.N. with responsibility for the occupation of Haiti. They plan to go in and get out as quickly as possible. And after two or three years of an Aristide presidency Haiti will be hell on earth.[27]

At the last moment, a direct U.S. invasion was averted. Through the intervention of former Pres. Jimmy Carter, Haitian military leaders agreed to cede power to Aristide, making a direct attack on the nation by U.S. forces unnecessary. Instead, U.S. forces arrived peacefully and worked with the Haitian military to arrange a transfer of power to Aristide. This process did not negate the flawed nature of the policy itself—an intervention on behalf of Marxist-oriented, violence-prone elements—but it did reduce the likelihood of American forces shedding their blood to accomplish this insidious goal.

Eventually, on cue, the U.N. Security Council decided to transfer the Haitian mission from U.S. to U.N. command, with the *Washington Post* explaining:

The United States insisted that an American command the force, but Maj. Gen. Joseph W. Kinzer will answer, technically at least, to the

political authority of U.N. Secretary General
Boutros Boutros-Ghali, not the Pentagon.[28]

The *Post* also reported that the rules of engagement were changing as a result of U.N. control of the operation. Now, the paper noted, U.S. forces would be permitted to open fire only when fired upon— "much more restrictive terms than those under which U.S. troops operated when they landed in Haiti." Now U.S. forces were becoming "United Nations fighting persons."

But, there was another curious aspect of the transfer of authority in Haiti. Initially, the administration had considered appointing Lt. Gen. Daniel Schroeder as the nominal head of U.N. troops in Haiti. But, his three-star rank meant that the Senate would have had to confirm his appointment. This was not the case with two-star General Kinzer.[29] Obviously, the Clinton administration was hoping to avoid any congressional scrutiny of its secretive policy.

Despite a crime wave and the assassination of a leading Aristide opponent, the Clinton administration was pronouncing the Haiti intervention as proof that U.N. peacekeeping can work after all. Clinton himself made a visit to the country to claim success. More than $1 million was spent in Operation Whitewash to repaint U.S. military vehicles with U.N. markings and outfit U.S. troops in blue helmets and berets and U.N. patches on their shoulders.[30]

However, the achilles heel in the policy of continuing to rely on the U.N. involves the failure of the United States to treat Americans involved in U.N. operations as American POW/MIAs when they are captured, kidnapped, or killed. This represents an unconscionable abandonment of our troops. Not surprisingly, this issue is of paramount concern to troops, veterans, and their families. It should also be a worry

for those Americans who want an armed forces that
will protect American and not foreign interests.

A ground-breaking article in *The American Legion
Magazine* by Miles Z. Epstein had noted that the first
such case actually dated back to 1983, when a navy
aviator participating in a peacekeeping mission under
U.S. control in Beirut, Lt. Robert O. Goodman, was
shot down while conducting an air raid over Syrian-
held territory in Lebanon. Goodman, who was captured by the Syrians, was classified as a hostage—not
a POW.

Such a designation was extremely controversial.
The article quoted attorney James H. Jeffries as saying, "To deny Goodman POW status removed him
from the highest protected status to a category with
no defined legal rights."[31] But, the same situation ap-
plies to rapidly expanding peacekeeping operations
under the control of the U.N. The magazine quoted
Lawrence J. Korb, a liberal defense expert at the
Brookings Institution, as saying that whenever peacekeeping or humanitarian missions are carried out
under a United Nations resolution, the Geneva Conventions should apply. Jeffries agreed. But, the reality
was something else. The magazine noted that the
Department of Defense had issued directive 1300.7
declaring that Americans deployed during peacetime—
such as during U.S. or U.N. peacekeeping operations—
are not protected by the Geneva Conventions. The
directive said that, "Since a state of armed conflict
does not exist, there is no protection afforded under
the Geneva Convention."[32]

Changing the directive internally within the Pentagon was certainly an option. Eliminating U.S. participation in nebulous and vague peacekeeping operations was another option. But, nothing was going to
stop the Clinton administration from going forward
with its world army scheme.

The issue remained unresolved, when the Clinton administration in May 1994, issued its pro-U.N. "Policy on Reforming Multilateral Peace Operations," based on a Presidential Decision Directive (PDD 25) that was classified as secret. Moreover, the U.S. Congress, the branch of government constitutionally responsible for declaring war and regulating the armed forces, was denied access to this secret pro-U.N. plan, as the following exchange during congressional hearing illustrated:

> Rep. Benjamin Gilman: "Madame Ambassador, on a number of occasions we've requested to see the actual document containing PDD 25. We've gotten some summaries, but thus far we haven't received any full documentation. Can you tell me when we can expect to see the full language of PDD 25?"

> Madeleine Albright, U.S. Ambassador to the U.N.: "Congressman Gilman, PDD 25 is an executive branch document that is never released to the Congressional side of the government."[33]

Despite the failure to release the actual text, the public document was portrayed by the administration and the media as a step backward from the scheme proposed by Boutros-Ghali. This document flatly stated, "The U.S. does not support a standing U.N. army." However, a Republican analysis of the public proposal noted that

> the Clinton plan lays the institutional groundwork for the future creation of such a force by calling for the creation by the U.N. of a Plans Division, an Information and Research Division, an Operations Division, a Logistical Division, a Public Affairs Cell, a Civil Police Cell, and a Professional Peace Operations Training Program. The U.N. should also have a "rapidly

deployable headquarters team" and its own "modest airlift capabilities."[34]

It appears the PDD 25 was nothing more than a go-slow approach to the world army plan. PDD 25 was, in fact, a reformulated version of a proposed PDD 13, whose partial contents were revealed by the *Washington Post* on 5 August 1993, and were seen as a blanket endorsement of Boutros-Ghali's standing army scheme. Members of Congress, as well as grassroots citizen organizations, had strongly protested it.

Despite some changes, however, the central purpose remained in PDD 25. According to the public version, the document unilaterally affirmed the president's authority as commander in chief "to place U.S. forces under the operational control of a foreign commander when doing so serves American security interests."[35] This was not an insignificant statement, and it is still not clear on what constitutional basis, if any, President Clinton is acting.

Moreover, the document went on to acknowledge that the administration had not yet figured out this critical issue of how to protect and defend what it now called "U.S. Peacekeepers"—U.S. troops involved in U.N. activities. The document said:

> The U.S. remains concerned that in some cases, captured U.N. peacekeepers and U.N. peace enforcers may not have adequate protection under international law. The U.S. believes that individuals captured while performing U.N. peace keeping or U.N. peace enforcement activities, whether as members of a U.N. force or a U.S. force executing a U.N. Security Council mandate, should, as a matter of policy, be immediately released to U.N. officials; until released at a minimum they should be accorded protections identical to those afforded prison-

ers of war under the 1949 Geneva Convention.
The U.S. will generally seek to incorporate
appropriate language into U.N. Security Council resolutions that establish or extend peace
operations in order to provide adequate legal
protection to captured U.N. peacekeepers. In
appropriate cases, the U.S. would seek assur-
ances that U.S. forces assisting the U.N. are
treated as experts on mission for the United
Nations, and thus are entitled to appropriate
privileges and immunities and are subject to
immediate release when captured. Moreover,
the Administration is actively involved in nego-
tiating a draft international convention at the
United Nations to provide a special international status for individuals serving in peacekeeping and peace enforcement operations under a U.N. mandate. Finally, the Administration will take appropriate steps to ensure that
any U.S. military personnel captured while serving as part of a multinational peacekeeping
force or peace enforcement effort are immediately released to U.N. authorities.[36]

The latter was a reference to what became the
"U.N. Convention on the Safety of U.N. and Associated Personnel," reported out of the U.N. General
Assembly and scheduled for submission for ratification by the U.S. Senate. This document attempts to
criminalize attacks on U.N. peacekeepers, such as
Durant in Somalia, by giving nation-states U.N. authorization to prosecute their kidnappers or attackers. In
other words, in typical fashion, the administration has
used the problem of the nonstatus as American POW/
MIAs of U.S. troops in U.N. operations to increase the
power of the U.N. even more.

None of this, of course, is necessary. It is just
another attempt to give the U.N. power over our troops

and, therefore, our nation. The Clinton administration itself undermined the case for U.S. involvement in U.N. military activities in June 1993, when on its own it authorized the U.S. Armed Forces to stage a missile attack on Iraq's intelligence headquarters, in retaliation for the attempted assassination of former President George Bush during his visit to Kuwait.

To be sure, the administration cited Article 51 of the U.N. Charter as justification for the raid. But, this provision is only supposed to guarantee nations the right to defend themselves against armed attack. Without the U.N. Charter, of course, the United States can accomplish the same thing and much more. The desire to refer to the charter, as if it confers legitimacy on a legitimate act of national defense, is the knee-jerk response of an administration that seems to be afraid or ashamed to defend U.S. security interests, or which is determined to enlarge the power and scope of the U.N. at the expense of American sovereignty.

The other danger for our troops, besides the lingering problem of their nonstatus as POW/MIAs in U.N. operations, involves the issue of whether the administration threatens to demoralize our forces by confusing them about whose interests they are supposed to protect and defend.

The potential problems surfaced in May 1994, when three hundred marines at the Twenty-nine Palms Marine Corps Base were asked some controversial questions about their attitudes about "nontraditional missions," such as U.N. peacekeeping operations. Some questions had to do with U.S. combat troops being used within the United States for missions involving drug enforcement, disaster relief, security at national events, environmental clean-up, teaching in public schools, community assistance, serving as federal and state prison guards, acting as a national emergency police force, serving as advisors to federal agencies, and border patrol. The marines were also asked whether they felt that U.S. combat troops under U.S. command should be used in other countries for similar tasks.

Regarding the U.N., the marines were asked for their reactions to a number of statements about whether U.S. and U.N. military operations should be integrated. The statements included:

> • U.S. combat troops should participate in U.N. missions under United Nations command and control.

> • It would make no difference to me to take orders from a U.N. company commander.

> • I feel the President of the United States has the authority to pass his responsibilities as Commander-in-Chief to the U.N. Secretary General.

> • I feel there is no conflict between my oath of office and serving as a U.N. soldier.

> • I would swear to the following code: "I am a United Nations fighting person. I serve in the forces which maintain world peace and every nation's way of life. I am prepared to give my life in their defense."[37]

Finally, these potential U.N. "fighting persons" were asked for their response to this one:

> The U.S. government declares a ban on the possession, sale, transportation, and transfer of all non-sporting firearms. A thirty (30) day amnesty period is permitted for these firearms to be turned over to the local authorities. At the end of this period, a number of citizen groups refuse to turn over their firearms. Consider the following statement: I would fire upon U.S. citizens who refuse or resist confiscation of firearms banned by the U.S. government.[38]

When word of the controversial survey leaked out, the Naval Postgraduate School Faculty issued a statement saying it was conducted by a U.S. naval officer in order to "study attitudes of military personnel who have been or might be placed in nontraditional missions." It said the survey was part of an independent master's thesis developed by the officer.

Just an academic exercise? Perhaps. But, it was significant that the school also said that the student's idea for the thesis originated from the Department of Defense's Bottom Up Review, an analysis of defense needs that included a section on peacekeeping, disaster relief, humanitarian assistance, and peace enforcement operations. The school also said the student's idea for the thesis came from considering the implications of Presidential Review Directives 13 and 25 "which directed DOD to create a U.S. military force structure whose command and control would include the United Nations."[39]

Whether the survey was an academic exercise or not, the hard fact remains that this student, with faculty guidance, considered it reasonable to ask American soldiers their reaction to the possibility that the U.N. might one day give orders to American forces to shoot Americans. This possibility, though "theoretical," is still extraordinary and ominous.

The press release said that one objective of the study was to "post hypothetical situations to assess a respondent's knowledge of the Uniform Code of Military Justice and the U.S. Constitution." But, this raises additional questions: Why are American troops being put in such a position in the first place? Why are such "hypothetical" questions necessary and how and why have we come to such a point?

Charles J. Dunlap, Jr., examined some of these hypothetical situations in an article appearing in the winter 1992-93 issue of *Parameters*, the U.S. Army War

College Quarterly. His article carried the striking title, "The Origins of the American Military Coup of 2012," and took the form of a letter from a senior retired officer of the "Unified Air Forces," arrested and convicted for opposing a coup that installs a general in the White House as "permanent Military Plenipotentiary."

In this letter, the officer argues that the coup "was the outgrowth of trends visible as far back as 1992," an apparent reference to Clinton administration actions affecting the armed forces. The letter outlined concern about "certain contemporary developments affecting the armed forces," such as Congress passing a "revised charter" for the armed forces, in which Congress "formalized" the process of having U.S. military forces engage in "humanitarian and nation-building assignments"—missions which "undermined the military's sense of itself" and left it isolated from society as a whole.[40] This is an obvious reference to the U.N.'s Somalia debacle.

Richard H. Kohn, former Chief of Air Force History for the U.S. Air Force, was astounded by the article, which appeared in the army's leading professional journal, even though it was supposed to be fictitious. The subject matter, he said, is "something officers never mention in public and barely ever whisper in private." Kohn's own article, published in the *National Interest*, carried the ominous headline, "Out of Control: The Crisis in Civil-Military Relations."[41]

Is any of this possible in real life? Gilbert A. Lewthwaite of the *Baltimore Sun* has reported that the American Armed Forces are, indeed, suffering from many problems today. He reports, "Almost a quarter-century after the end of the draft, military analysts warn that the all-volunteer forces are becoming increasingly isolated from a civilian society that is less likely to share their experiences, values or concerns."

He added that observers such as former Navy Secretary John F. Lehman, Jr., suggest that the rift they see developing "could eventually erode the nation's long-time civilian control over the military."[42] Some of these complicating factors, he reported, include "the human difficulties of downsizing" the military and coping with "new roles and missions in the post-Cold War era," an obvious reference to U.N.-style activities.

Events may be moving faster than many of us think. In order to be an effective world government, the U.N. has to have a world army, as well as a court system to prosecute criminals, such as those hypothetical Americans who resist confiscation of their firearms. In fact, the U.N. Security Council had already passed a resolution creating an international tribunal to prosecute those responsible for war crimes in Bosnia and other former Yugoslav republics.

Some see this as worthwhile. Futurist John Naisbitt saw the Bosnia tribunal as a positive development, "the first international court empowered to try crimes against humanity since the Nuremberg trials of Nazis after World War II."[43] It is understandable why people want to see the perpetrators of war crimes brought to justice. However, analyst C. Douglas Lummis says there is absolutely no basis in law or the U.N. Charter for such a tribunal. He says it was established by Security Council resolutions. But, that

> answers nothing. Where does the Security Council get such power? The legal fiction is that the power comes from Chapter VII of the U.N. Charter. Chapter VII authorizes the U.N. to deploy the armed forces of member states in peacekeeping operations. Stretch the words as you will, you cannot make them say that the U.N. has the power to put people in jail under criminal charges. On the contrary, the Charter,

written by representatives of states jealous of their power, falls all over itself to insist that the U.N. may never usurp the sovereign rights of states.[44]

Lummis points out that a comparison between this tribunal and the Nuremberg and Tokyo trials is faulty, because the latter were military tribunals, "carried out by conquering powers in territories under their direct rule." The U.N. tribunal, by contrast, is exercising unwarranted power "to prosecute individuals from states that still retain their sovereign independence." Nevertheless, this tribunal has been in operation and even maintains jail cells.

Lummis comments:

> If the U.N. takes on the powers to arrest, prosecute, sentence and imprison individuals, it is taking on sovereign powers hitherto reserved to states. Add to this Secretary General Boutros Boutros-Ghali's proposal that the U.N. have its own permanent military arm, and you have the conditions for a full-fledged world state.[45]

This tribunal appears to be just the first step in an unfolding process that could threaten real and not just hypothetical American citizens. In fact, writing in *Constitution* magazine, Benjamin B. Ferencz described the tribunal as possibly a "stepping stone to a permanent court."[46]

None of this was ever supposed to transpire. Former Senator Goldwater noted that when the U.N. was established, there was serious opposition to U.N. involvement in any judicial proceedings that could affect member states:

> When the United Nations Charter was under consideration in San Francisco in 1945, the proposal to establish a World Court—with com-

pulsory jurisdiction over the member states—created a stumbling block which threatened to prevent widespread acceptance of the U.N. Charter. Ultimately a compromise was reached. The International Court of Justice was to function only in accordance with a so-called "statute," annexed to the Charter and made a part thereof. Though all members of the United Nations were declared to be parties to the statute and might therefore voluntarily resort to the Court for settlement of any particular international dispute, no nation is subject to the general compulsory jurisdiction of the Court except to the extent that it may so agree in a formal declaration deposited with the Secretary General of the United Nations.[47]

The currently functioning International Court of Justice must not be confused with the plans for an International Criminal Court that are being finalized right now by the Clinton administration.

From all indications, this court would have compulsory jurisdiction, including over American citizens.

Notes

1. Maj. Joseph F. Napoli, "Current U.N. Bashing Trend Is Way Off Base," *Army Times* (10 April 1995): 31.

2. John Naisbitt, *Global Paradox* (New York: Avon Books, 1994), 202.

3. Barbara Crossette, "U.N. Chief Chides Security Council on Military Missions," *New York Times* (6 January 1995): 3.

4. "The Peace Powers Act of 1995," Testimony of Senate Majority Leader Bob Dole, Senate Committee on Foreign Relations, 21 March 1995.

5. Will Marshall and Martin Schram, *Mandate for Change* (New York: Berkeley Books, 1993), 306.

6. Boutros Boutros-Ghali, "An Agenda for Peace," report of the secretary general pursuant to the statement adopted by the Summit Meeting of the Security Council on 31 January 1992 (New York: United Nations, 1992), 25.

7. Strobe Talbott, "The Birth of the Global Nation," *Time* (20 July 1992): 70.

8. As quoted in *The Howard Phillips Issues and Strategy Bulletin* (15 September 1993): 1.

9. As quoted by Sen. Paul Coverdell, "Charting a Clear Foreign Policy Course," *Washington Times* (4 January 1994): A14.

10. As quoted in Paul A. Gigot, "Defense Fight: GOP Shouldn't Sink to 'Borking,' " *Wall Street Journal* (10 September 1993).

11. Robin L. Higgins, letter to *USA Today* (19 March 1993).

12. Robin L. Higgins, Speech to Mayor's Breakfast, Veterans Day, 6 November 1993.

13. Ibid.

14. Keith B. Richburg, "U.N. Mission in Somalia Beset by Infiltrators," *Washington Post* (7 September 1993).

15. As quoted by Anne Marie Kilday, "2 Texas Congressmen Call for Resignation of Aspin," *Dallas Morning News* (29 October 1993): 8a.

16. As quoted in "Update," Hillsdale College, vol. 4, no. 2, 2.

17. Keith B. Richburg, "Somalia Slips Back to Bloodshed," *Washington Post* (4 September 1994): 1.

18. Aden Ali, Reuters News Agency, *Washington Times* (15 January 1995): A7.

19. Jeane Kirkpatrick, "Sticky Foam Doesn't Belong in Marine Arsenal," *Conservative Chronicle* (1 March 1995): 28.

20. Ibid.

21. Al Kamen, "Who's In Charge on Bosnia Anyway?" *Washington Post* (18 February 1994).

22. Sen. Paul Coverdell, news release, 16 February 1994.

23. David Rieff, "The Peacekeepers Who Couldn't," *Washington Post* (11 December 1994): C1.

24. "Haiti, the U.N. and the Monroe Doctrine," Republican Research Committee, (8 August 1994): 1.

25. "Haiti Documents," Congressional Research Service, undated.

26. Ibid.

27. Ibid.

28. Julia Preston, "U.N. Council Sets Command Shift for Haiti Mission," *Washington Post* (31 January 1995): A21.

29. "What Was The Mission of Sgt. Cardott?" *Washington Times* (16 January 1995): editorial.

30. Douglas Farah, "Helmets Repainted in Haiti but U.N. Can't Paper Over Problems," *Washington Post* (4 April 1995): A32.

31. Miles Z. Epstein, "How Far Should America Go To Bring Them Home?" *American Legion Magazine* (March 1993): 25.

32. Ibid., 26.

33. Hearing of the International Security, International Organizations and Human Rights Subcommittee of the House Foreign Affairs Committee, Tensions in U.S.-U.N. Relations, 17 May 1994.

34. "Clinton's U.N. Peacekeeping Plan Still Flawed," Republican Research Committee, undated.

35. "The Clinton Administration's Policy on Reforming Multilateral Peace Operations," White House (May 1994): 2.

36. Ibid., 22.

37. "Combat Arms Survey," received 19 May 1994.

38. Ibid.

39. "Subject: Survey of Marines on the Use of Military Forces in Non-traditional Missions," John Sanders, Public Affairs officer, Naval Postgraduate School, 3 August 1994.

40. Charles J. Dunlap, Jr., "The Origins of the American Military Coup of 2012," *Parameters* (Winter, 1992–93): 2–20.

41. Richard K. Kohn, "Out of Control: The Crisis in Civil-Military Relations," *National Interest* (Spring 1994): 3–17.

42. Gilbert A. Lewthwaite, "Military Growing Isolated from Society, Analysts Say," *Baltimore Sun* (12 December 1994): 1.

43. John Naisbitt, *Global Paradox* (New York: Avon Books, 1994), 202.

44. C. Douglas Lummis, "Time To Watch the Watchers," *Nation* (26 September 1994): 302.

45. Ibid., 302.

46. Benjamin B. Ferencz, "Needed: An International Criminal Court," *Constitution* (Fall 1993).

47. Barry M. Goldwater, *Why Not Victory* (New York: McGraw-Hill, 1962), 102, 103.

The U.N.

3

Constitutional Crisis

The American system of constitutional government is under unprecedented assault. President Clinton has unilaterally abandoned his role as commander in chief to the U.N. and the Congress has failed to impeach him for it. In this crucial period, with the nation at a crossroads, it is important for the American people to put tremendous pressure on Congress to reassert control over our national sovereignty.

The Congress should not sit back. The American people would be on their side in this dispute. On 2 November 1993, the Times Mirror Center for the People & The Press released the results of a survey on foreign policy issues that was very bad news for the Clinton administration and other proponents of the U.N. world army scheme. It found that the American people by a huge margin (69 percent vs. 25 percent) rejected the concept of putting U.S. military forces under U.N. command. The findings demonstrated that the American people take a lot of pride in their armed forces and do not want to see their military personnel turned over to a foreign body.

By contrast, the survey found that as many as four-fifths of Americans it called "influentials," including supposed "experts" in foreign affairs and Washington journalists, favored the concept of "placing American troops in a permanent force under United Nations command."

Interestingly, the survey found that members of both major political parties favored assigning U.S. troops to the U.N., although Democrats were far more inclined toward this policy than Republicans (81 percent vs. 55 percent) and liberals were far more willing than conservatives (87 percent vs. 48 percent).[1] The findings indicate that a significant percentage of those against deployment of U.S. forces in U.N. military operations are independents who provide an important swing vote during presidential contests.

The Republican party, being more conservative than the Democratic party, tried to take political advantage of public sentiment on this issue by campaigning for seats in the House of Representatives on the basis of a document, the "Contract with America," which attempted to reduce U.S. reliance on the U.N. The main authors of the plan were House Speaker Newt Gingrich and House Majority Leader Dick Armey.

In the section of the contract affirming a "Strong National Defense," the authors asserted:

> Isn't national defense the first and foremost priority of the federal government? For forty years prior to the fall of the Berlin Wall, Americans stood shoulder to shoulder against international communism—and we won. But with the end of the Cold War, some have taken to raiding the defense budget to fund social welfare programs and UN peacekeeping programs. Our defense forces have been cut so deeply that we risk a return to the "hollow military" of the 1970s. And for the first time in our history, American troops have been placed under UN command.[2]

The latter was a reference to the Somalia operation, in which the U.N., with President Clinton's acquiescence, took control of U.S. forces. In opposing such schemes, which are indeed based on raiding the defense budget and depleting our troops of military readiness funds, the Republicans did not precisely charge that the president had violated the U.S. Constitution. Yet, the Constitution is quite clear, with Article II, Section 2, saying, "The President shall be Commander in Chief of the Army and Navy of the United States." It says "shall be," not may or could be, and does not permit the president to relinquish this authority or cede it to another body or individual.

The Republican contract seemed unambiguous. It stated that they were going to vote a flat prohibition on the placement of U.S. troops under U.N. command. The subtitle of one section in the contract was explicitly titled "Prohibition of Foreign Command of U.S. Armed Forces." It couldn't get much clearer than that. The actual wording declared, "We would prohibit the Defense Department from taking part in military operations that place U.S. troops under foreign command." But, it then described a loophole:

> The President may waive this provision if he certifies to Congress that operational control of our troops under foreign command is vital to our national security interests.[3]

But, this wasn't the only loophole. Under another subtitle, "Placing U.S. Troops Under Foreign Command for U.N. Peacekeeping Activities," the document expressly allowed placement of U.S. troops under U.N. command if Congress approved it.

On the Senate side, Majority Leader Robert Dole introduced the Peace Powers Act of 1995, another worthwhile attempt to move Clinton away from his reliance on the U.N. Like the contract, though, it contained a loophole—allowing the president to put U.S. troops under foreign command for U.N. peace-keeping if the president assured Congress it is in the national interest. Former U.S. Ambassador to the U.N., Jeane Kirkpatrick, said the bill should have gone further:

> To the Dole bill's provisions, which might only regularize and institutionalize assignment of U.S. forces whenever a President certifies that it serves the national interest, I would prefer a simple prohibition. It is the only way, I suspect, to save U.S. armed forces from being assigned to dangerous situations, inadequately armed and incompetently commanded while operating under U.N. rules of engagement.[4]

The congressional Republican response to Clinton's formation of a world army under U.N. auspices was described as weak by two Republican lawyers who had served in the Reagan and Bush administrations, Lee A. Casey and David B. Rivkin. They commented that:

> Contrary to the claims of its critics, the [Dole] bill's major flaw is not that it would prohibit the president from assigning American forces to U.N. command, but that it purports to allow such arrangements if Congress gives it consent. Under the Constitution, the president does not have the authority, either as commander-in-chief or as chief executive, to subordinate American troops to foreign command—and Congress cannot vest him with that authority.[5]

Furthermore, Casey and Rivkin noted that the Constitution, through its Appointments Clause (Article II, Section 2), contained a legal requirement that anyone exercising the legal authority of the United States be an "officer" of the United States. They added:

> Although the Appointments Clause is more often analyzed in terms of civilian appointments, it is fully applicable to military appointments. . . . Indeed, it is difficult to think of a more significant federal authority than the right to command American troops and, unlike the civilian service, Congress has required that even very junior military officers be appointed by and with the consent of the Senate. Neither the president nor Congress can waive the applicability of the Appointments Clause. As a result, no individual, whether the secretary general of the United Nations or a U.N. commander in the field, who is not a properly appointed officer of the United States can direct the actions of American troops.[6]

It appears that Republican lawmakers were reluctant to state forthright that the president had already behaved in an unconstitutional manner and might, therefore, be subject to impeachment. Perhaps the Republicans were unwilling to make this case and provoke a possible constitutional crisis. As a result, their proposals to redress this unprecedented presidential action fall short of what is constitutionally required.

Interestingly, some Democrats seemed to recognize that the president had gone too far. Sen. Joseph Biden, for example, had introduced a congressional resolution allowing American troops to be part of a standing army controlled by the U.N. At least Senator Biden seemed to think that congressional action of some sort was necessary before Clinton turned his constitutional powers over to Boutros-Ghali.[7] Biden's mistake was in thinking Congress had the power to turn our forces over to the U.N.

The Constitution is quite clear about the responsibilities of both the president and the Congress. Under Article I, Section 8, the Congress is given the power to declare war, create an army and navy, and make rules and regulations for the armed forces. There is no provision for ceding control of the military to foreigners. And, there is no provision for Congress to enable the commander in chief to abandon his constitutional role or for the president to do that on his own.

In the version of the contract that passed the House, however, the National Security Revitalization Act did not contain the provision requiring the president to seek advance congressional approval for placing U.S. troops under U.N. command. Instead, it simply required the president to describe the mission and certify in advance that putting U.S. forces under U.N. command would be in the national interest. This was similar to the language in the Dole bill.

It is not entirely clear what congressional Republicans are attempting to do by requiring the president to certify that his actions are in the national interest. Clinton himself, in the PDD 25, said he would only assign U.S. troops to the U.N. in cases of the national interest. This is boilerplate language that any politician will use. It's difficult—if not impossible—to conceive of any circumstances under which a president would admit his actions were *not* in the national interest. Perhaps the GOP effort was simply an attempt to somehow inhibit the president from acting in an unconstitutional manner. In any case, it wasn't good enough.

The failure to challenge the unconstitutional abdication of presidential responsibility and flatly prohibit U.S. military involvement with the U.N. meant that the Republicans created another problem they had to address. The contract said that Republican legislation would express the belief of

> Congress that the President should take all necessary steps to (1) ensure that any U.S. military personnel captured during UN peace-keeping activities are to be treated as prisoners of war and (2) bring to justice all individuals responsible for the mistreatment, torture, and death of American prisoners.[8]

This section was an acknowledgment that U.S. troops involved in U.N. operations do not become American POW/MIAs when they are missing or captured. It means they enter a kind of legal limbo. However, a "sense of Congress" resolution is meaningless, especially when the president is pursuing a policy already at variance with the Constitution itself. Asking the president for action on such an important matter is a very poor substitute for Congress taking action itself.

Meanwhile, the Clinton administration and the U.N. took advantage of this vacuum in policy to help draft a new international agreement giving "U.S. peace-keepers" a vague new status. A treaty called the Convention on the Safety of United Nations and Associated Personnel was adopted by the U.N. General Assembly and was scheduled for submission to the U.S. Senate. If ratified, it will confirm the status of American troops in U.N. operations as something other than American POW/MIAs when captured, attacked, or killed. The new policy will give U.N. authority to the United States and other nation-states to pursue those who attack, capture, or kill "U.N. fighting persons."

None of this would be necessary if Congress would simply vote a flat prohibition on U.N. support for U.N. peacekeeping. The Republicans did not propose

to do this, either. However, they did propose to stop
the Clinton administration practice of raiding the
budget of the Department of Defense to pay for esca-
lating costs of U.N. peacekeeping activities. This resulted in a drain of at least $1 billion from the Pen-
tagon in 1994. The *Army Times* newspaper noted, "In
1994, readiness accounts were so depleted by unex-
pected operations that some training exercises had to
be canceled, some aircraft units were grounded and
readiness was allowed to decline in three Army divi-
sions." In 1995, the amount of money drained from
readiness accounts was expected to be $2.5 billion.[9]

Republicans, to their credit, knew this was happening and strongly protested. Responding to their
criticism, on 13 October 1994, during a Department
of Defense press briefing, Deputy Defense Secretary
John Deutch said that the readiness of our forces was
"higher" than it was before the Persian Gulf War and
that our forces "are ready, and more ready and capable than they've ever been."

Congressman Floyd Spence, the ranking minority
member of the House Armed Services Committee who
became chairman of the renamed House National
Security Committee after the elections, had concrete
evidence proving Deutch wrong. He fired off a letter
to Defense Secretary William Perry detailing serious
readiness problems that were known months before
Deutch made his statement. Perry subsequently acknowledged that Spence was right, and that the Pentagon had to cut drastically into military training during the summer and fall of 1994 because readiness
funds were being diverted into "non-traditional missions" such as U.N. "world army" operations.

In response to these astonishing disclosures,
Deutch said that he was unaware of the problems
when he made his remarks on October 13. Unaware?
Deutch was the number two man in the Pentagon; he

was in a position to know, should have known, and probably did know. The fact is that his comments in October were intended to counter Republican election-eve charges that the Clinton administration was concealing a readiness problem. Secretary Perry's admission that the Republicans were right came conveniently *after* the election. For misleading the American people and the Congress, Deutch was rewarded with a nomination as CIA Director, for which he demanded cabinet-level rank.

The GOP contract noted that the Clinton administration was taking this readiness money out of the defense budget for the U.N. without any congressional authorization, implying that the president was behaving in a possibly illegal or unconstitutional manner. Again, however, the Republicans refused to make this charge directly. Similarly, Senator Dole, in testimony on behalf of his own Peace Powers Act, described what was happening:

> The U.S. representative to the United Nations routinely votes to establish, extend and expand operations long after congressional appropriations have been exhausted. In most other government programs, this would be illegal. At the least, it is unwise. Billions of dollars of U.S. costs in direct and indirect support of U.N. peacekeeping have been accumulated, yet the administration refuses to even seek credit toward the U.S. assessment [of U.N. dues].[10]

Incredibly, Dole said that figures from the Government Accounting Office revealed that these costs from fiscal year 1992 to fiscal year 1995 exceeded $10 billion—more than three times what members of Congress thought the United States was spending on U.N. peacekeeping.

The U.N. funding proposal, in its final form as

part of the House National Security Revitalization Act, simply required that additional U.S. support for U.N. peacekeeping be counted as part of the regular U.S. contribution to the world body. The same provision was in the Dole bill. The Republicans were essentially settling for trying to eliminate what House Speaker Gingrich described as "double-billing" by the U.N. In effect, the Republicans were asking that Clinton spend only that money appropriated by Congress. Even this mild provision, however, was strongly attacked by Clinton administration officials who said it would somehow break the U.N. financially and force existing U.N. peacekeeping operations to shut down. Indeed, Clinton threatened to veto the bill.

Ironically, Clinton had taken the high ground on an issue when he should have been begging the forgiveness of the American people for sending their sons and daughters into dangerous and misguided U.N. missions. He was threatening Congress at a time when Congress should have been threatening his impeachment.

Unfortunately, House Republicans also failed to insist on a provision in their contract that would have greatly restricted U.S. intelligence-sharing with the U.N. After Clinton officials claimed no secrets had been lost through the world body, House Republicans "watered down" this provision in their final bill.

It was subsequently revealed in a dramatic front page *Washington Post* article that boxes of secret documents were left behind in vacant U.N. offices in Somalia that included "source reports" or interviews with Somali informers who could easily have ended up dead as a result of U.N. incompetence. Some of the documents, officials told the paper, were marked "NOFORN," meaning no dissemination to foreigners, and yet they were found in the hands of U.N. intelligence officials led by a Nigerian colonel.[11] Senator

Dole, House Speaker Gingrich, and other congressional leaders responded to this by asking Clinton to immediately suspend intelligence sharing with the U.N.

The entire controversy demonstrated to what extent the Clinton administration has been conspiring with U.N. officials to construct a world army with U.S. troops paid for largely by U.S. taxpayers. It also showed that the administration realized that U.N. military operations involving U.S. troops were so unpopular with the American people that they could not get approved and funded in advance by Congress.

Overall, the Republican legislation went in the right direction. But, it remains a cause for concern why they didn't go further. The Republicans took control of Congress saying that a key message of the electorate was a desire for smaller government. Yet, their proposals having to do with the U.N. mostly amounted to cosmetic changes in the way the United States interacted with the world body.

In the final analysis, the case has to be made that U.S. withdrawal is the only way to safeguard the precious heritage—national sovereignty—left to us by the founding fathers. Of the two major parties, only the Republicans seem capable of making this case. But, it might require a constitutional confrontation between the Republican Congress and a Democratic president— or election of a conservative Republican president—to make real progress.

Meantime, what can be accomplished is full-scale congressional hearings into how previous administrations, mostly Democratic, got the United States entangled in the world body and laid the groundwork for the Clinton/Boutros-Ghali world army scheme. Such hearings could lay the groundwork for a renewed assault on those eager to build up U.N. military forces at the expense of our troops.

Such hearings would reveal that a proposal for a

U.N. peace force or world army actually dates back to
1961, when the U.S. Department of State under the
Kennedy administration issued a document entitled
*Freedom from War: The United States Program for General
and Complete Disarmament in a Peaceful World.*[12] This
extraordinary document, introduced at the Sixteenth
General Assembly of the United Nations, urged:

> The disbanding of all national armed forces
> and the prohibition of their reestablishment in
> any form whatsoever other than those required
> to preserve internal order and for contribu-
> tions to a United Nations Peace Force.[13]

There is no question about the authenticity of this
document; the Arms Control and Disarmament Agency
of the State Department confirms its legitimacy. And,
it wasn't just a report issued by a faceless bureaucrat
that got lost on a shelf somewhere. Dated September
1961, it was submitted in response to U.N. General
Assembly Resolution 1378 of 20 November 1959,
advocating "General and Complete Disarmament." A
subsequent General Assembly Resolution 1722, dated
20 December 1961, on a "Question of Disarmament,"
noted "with satisfaction" that both the U.S. and the
Soviets had submitted reports on the matter, and urged
that disarmament be carried out.

The U.S. endorsement of this scheme has apparently never been officially repudiated. In fact, the U.N.
and its allies in this country regard it as valid today.
Eric Cox, executive director of the Campaign for U.N.
Reform, says that the guiding principles of the U.S.
and Soviet documents, including that of a U.N. peace
force, became known as the McCloy-Zorin agreement,
named after John J. McCloy of the U.S. and Valerian
A. Zorin of the U.S.S.R. McCloy had been the chief
disarmament adviser and negotiator for President
Kennedy. Cox explained:

These principles were never implemented, but
this agreement was the closest the two superpowers and the world have come to recogniz-
ing the requirements for a world with no offensive weapons and an upgraded United Nations with an international peace force capable
of assuring world peace. The Cuban missile
crisis, the assassination of President Kennedy
and the removal of Nikita S. Krushchev from
power were among the reasons the McCloy-
Zorin approach to peace was not implemented.
The amazing thing is that the superpowers
acceded to a timetable leading to disarmament
and to a United Nations empowered to assure
world peace.[14]

Over the years, proponents of the U.N. or world
government have urged the United States to resurrect
and implement the U.N.-sponsored agreement.
Sandford Zee Persons, vice president of the World
Federalists, noted in 1983 that liberal Democratic Rep.
George Brown had introduced a resolution with thirty-
nine cosponsors asking the Reagan administration to
"initiate renewed serious consideration" of the agreement and "to initiate joint reconsideration" with the
Soviet Union on how to implement it.[15]

Implementation of such an agreement would probably have meant that we would have lost the Cold
War. The Reagan administration's major foreign policy
actions and successes, such as anti-Communist actions
in Grenada, Afghanistan, Angola, and Nicaragua, were
carried out without the approval of the U.N. Similarly,
the Bush administration intervened in Panama without getting approval from the U.N. It's doubtful, of
course, whether any of these operations would have
been approved by the U.N. The Reagan foreign policy
was also characterized by a massive build-up of U.S.

military forces, including development of the Strategic Defense Initiative (SDI), not the "disarmament" called for in McCloy-Zorin.

Aware that the pro-world government policy envisioned in McCloy-Zorin would never stand a chance of passing through any Congress, Democratic or Republican, the Clinton administration and the U.N. have simply resurrected the plan on their own. This is an unprecedented grab for political power and assault on our constitutional system of government. It's time for Congress to put a stop to it.

The election of a Republican Congress certainly represents an obstacle to their plans. The White House and U.N. supporters especially fear that anti-U.N. sentiment will grow in Congress, sparked by grassroots opposition to the U.N. and its schemes.

Indeed, the mere fact that Republicans came to power was enough to scare the U.N. and the White House. In a dispatch dated after the elections, *New York Times* reporter Barbara Crossette noted:

> For two years the Clinton Administration has been promising to rejoin UNESCO [The U.N. Education, Scientific and Cultural Organization]. . . . The United States left the agency in 1984, charging it with mismanagement and anti-Western bias.
>
> The money needed to make the move—about $65 million for the first year's dues—was in the State Department's 1996 budget request, which went to the White House this fall. . . .
>
> But after the November elections, when Republicans critical of the United Nations were catapulted into influential positions in Congress, the allocation for UNESCO membership was quietly dropped in a White House budget review.[16]

The November 1994 election victory represented not only an opportunity for the Republicans to keep the United States out of UNESCO but to seek complete U.S. withdrawal from the world body, on an incremental basis if need be. Failure to pursue such a course undoubtedly stems from the notion, popular even among some "moderate" Republicans, that people against the U.N. are right-wing nuts not worthy of serious attention. It's true that the liberal media regularly run articles suggesting that only a few political fringe elements oppose the organization. An article in the *New York Times Magazine*, for example, reported on Americans fleeing to Idaho to escape the oppression of government, including a few who were arming themselves against a "one world government" sponsored by the U.N. This view was presented as the ravings of a paranoid victim of conspiracy theories peddled by the far Right. Most U.N. opponents are dismissed as members of the John Birch Society, a controversial anti-Communist group that proclaims the catchy slogan: "Get the U.S. out of the U.N. and the U.N. out of the U.S."

But, these anti-U.N. views are not seen as so kooky anymore. After all, one U.N. agency, the U.N. Development Program, is openly proclaiming the goal of world government in its own publications and the U.N. is developing the mechanisms that would enable it to function as a world government, including a world army, police powers, a criminal court, jails and taxing authority.

The Republicans may have underestimated the extent of grassroots disgust and anger over what the U.N. represents—a transfer of powers delegated to the people by the Constitution to more distant levels of government, this time on an international level. There are broad sections of the American people—veterans, pro-family and anti-tax activists and just old-fashioned patriots—who are speaking out against the U.N. and even organizing against its growing influence in U.S. domestic and foreign affairs.

As Clinton, for example, proceeded with plans to integrate U.S. military forces into the U.N., grassroots citizens groups collected literally tens of thousands of names on petitions, which were delivered to the White House and Congress, protesting the scheme. Moreover, veterans groups, state legislative bodies, and even townships adopted resolutions urging the United States to cut off funding for U.N. military operations.

More importantly, Americans are taking to the streets to protest the world body. In early 1995, about twenty angry residents turned out to protest a decision to fly the U.N. flag at the City Hall in Gainesville, Florida. On United Nations Day, 24 October 1994, patriotic groups across the nation emerged "to protest what they see as the international body's growing influence on U.S. domestic and foreign policy," as the *Washington Times* put it. The *Times*, the conservative daily in the nation's capital, was one of the few news organizations to cover these activities.

In other incidents, protests occurred in Lansing, Michigan, where city officials planned to fly the U.N. flag outside City Hall. In Albuquerque, New Mexico, people staged demonstrations and letter writing campaigns to protest the decision by a state judge to fly the U.N. flag in his courtroom.

Back in October 1993, after U.S. troops in a U.N.-controlled military operation in Somalia were massacred in the streets, about forty members of the conservative youth group, Young Americans for Freedom, staged a demonstration in Costa Mesa, California, during which they burned a U.N. flag.

Anti-U.N. sentiment is reflected in many other ways. Pope John Paul II's opposition to the September 1994 U.N. Conference on Population and Development, which pursued an agenda of population control through abortion, helped alert millions of Catholics to the U.N.'s insidious plans. And, the pope was joined in his opposition to the U.N. by many prominent Americans, Catholics and non-Catholics, and their organizations. These included Dr. James C. Dobson, president, Focus on the Family; Robert P. Dugan, Jr., director, Office of Public Affairs, National Association of Evangelicals; Ralph Reed, executive director, Christian Coalition; Gary L. Bauer, president, Family Research Council; Allan Carlson, president, the Rockford Institute; Thomas V. Wykes, executive director, Catholic Campaign for America; Mercedes Arzu Wilson, Family of the Americas Foundation; James A. Miller, Population Research Institute and Father Paul Marx of Human Life International.

But, the reaction to the U.N. population conference was really nothing new. Conservative groups over the years have had to devote a significant amount of their time and effort to fighting dangerous U.N. treaties and conferences. This is energy that could have been expended opposing liberal policy proposals on Capitol Hill or implementing conservative initiatives.

For example, Phyllis Schlafly's Eagle Forum and Dr. James Dobson's Focus on the Family mounted major campaigns against the so-called U.N. Convention on the Rights of the Child, a dangerous measure that affirms more government involvement in child-rearing, while Dr. Beverly LaHaye's Concerned Women for America worked hard to expose the U.N. Convention on the Elimination of All Forms of Discrimination Against Women, another nice-sounding but insidious measure.

The Clinton administration's decision not to rejoin UNESCO was a victory for these conservative groups. Another positive impact of the Republican takeover of Congress was that U.N. proposals such as

the Convention on Biological Diversity and the Law of
the Sea Treaty were clearly going to have a difficult if
not impossible time moving through the Senate.

But, the Republicans must go further. After a series of congressional hearings exploring the U.N.'s
emergence as a proto-world government, Republicans
should come up with a plan to withdraw the United
States from the U.N. The Cato Institute, a libertarian-
oriented think tank, suggested four initial steps in a
handbook it prepared for the 104th Congress:

> pass legislation that prohibits U.S. troops from
> serving in U.N. military operations,
>
> refuse to ratify the Law of the Sea Treaty and
> reject similar schemes if they arise,
>
> reduce U.S. funding of the United Nations by
> 50 percent and consider even deeper cuts after
> that initial phase,
>
> encourage the Clinton Administration to ini-
> tiate negotiations to roll back the U.N. empire
> so that it is confined to a diplomatic–rather
> than a governing–role.[17]

The Cato plan is a good start. But, even a 50
percent cut in U.S. funding of the U.N. would leave
the international body a formidable bureaucracy. If
the United States withdrew, however, it would prove
to be a significant boon for domestic conservative
groups, freeing up their resources and enabling them
to concentrate their energy on Congress and the presidency.

Whatever the reason for the Republican decision
not to pursue this course so far, they have blown a
political opportunity, a decision they may come to
regret.

Political analyst Kevin Phillips has pointed out that
the 1919–20 Republican Congress emphasized issues

such as opposition to the U.N. predecessor, the League of Nations, Americanism and immigration control. As a result, the GOP in 1920 won the White House and scored big in Congress, with sixty-one more seats in the House and ten more in the Senate. By contrast, the Republican Congress of 1947–48 cooperated with the Democratic White House on a bipartisan foreign policy and concentrated on labor and tax policy, issues that were portrayed by the Democrats as favoritism to the rich. The result: President Truman upset Republican nominee Thomas Dewey, and the Republicans lost nine seats in the Senate and seventy-five in the House.[18]

The key to these outcomes, Phillips argues, is the independent populist vote, which can go either Democratic or Republican, depending on the election issues and themes. Populist voters are concerned about too much internationalism in American foreign policy and big business or Wall Street influence in politics. In 1996, there seems to be little chance of this vote going Democratic, since the Clinton administration is so committed to the U.N. and tied to Wall Street interests. But, the populist vote could leave the Republican party if a third party candidate emerges who appeals to this constituency. Such a candidate could easily argue that it is pure double-talk to insist that Americans can enjoy smaller government—a GOP campaign promise—while the United Nations continues to grow in power and influence over us.

Of the current crop of GOP contenders, Patrick J. Buchanan has taken on the U.N. most forcefully. But Sen. Bob Dole, a World War II veteran, and Sen. Phil Gramm have also been critical of the world body.

Regardless of what happens on the presidential level, Republicans in Congress would be well-advised to examine how the United States has gotten into this

U.N. trap and how to get out. A plan for withdrawal from the U.N. should be made a part of the 1996 Republican party platform.

Fifty years ago, when the organization was formed, many prominent Republicans supported it. Indeed, one of America's greatest anti-Communists, Minnesota Republican Congressman Walter Judd, was a strong booster. According to his biographer, Lee Edwards, Judd

> was a great and early supporter of the United Nations. In fact, in 1943, as a freshman Congressman, he was a co-sponsor of a resolution declaring that the United States should cooperate with other nations after World War II to bring into being "a world organization" through which peaceloving nations could pool their strength against lawless or aggressive actions by any nation. During the summer of 1943, Dr. Judd went on the road to give the case for a "world organization" and to mobilize public support for this new body.[19]

However, Judd became extremely concerned about the possibility that Communist China would be admitted to the U.N. He was one of the key organizers of the Committee of One Million against admission of Communist China to the U.N., a group that collected one million signatures on petitions. The main argument against China's admission was that China had played a major role in the Korean War and didn't deserve membership in a body whose members were supposed to be dedicated to keeping the peace.

But, the Soviet Union and many Third World nations backed China in increasing numbers over the years, to the point where on 25 October 1971, the U.N. General Assembly voted seventy-six to thirty-five to seat the Communists and evict the free Chinese.

This was a critical turning point and a major setback for the United States. Now there were two major Communist powers on the U.N. Security Council. The acknowledged leader of conservatives at the time, Republican Sen. Barry M. Goldwater, said that if Communist China were admitted, the United States should "suspend its political and financial support of the United Nations." Goldwater explained:

> Only by exercising that independence of action, even in so drastic a way as I now propose, do we continue to discharge our duty as leader and most powerful member of the free community of nations. By refusing to use the resources at our disposal, we reject our responsibilities, forfeit our strength, and weaken our cause.

> The Soviet Union often talks about boycotting the United Nations. In fact it has not done so. But that moment when withdrawal could be shown to advance the fortunes of the Soviet revolution, the Russians would walk out. It is every nation's sovereign right to withdraw from an international body. But the point is to exercise that right, not as the Soviet Union might, as the weapon of an aggressor, but as a nation must if its vital interests are at stake.[20]

The admission of Communist China was significant for another reason. In his subsequent book, *With No Apologies*, Goldwater put part of the blame on the U.N. for the failure to achieve total victory in the Korean conflict against the Chinese- and Russian-backed North Korean Communists, who had launched an unprovoked attack on South Korea. Goldwater said that while a U.N. resolution was cited as justification to intervene against the Communists, the U.N. itself

had to be understood as a key reason why total victory
over the aggressor was not achieved. He explained:

> The Security Council of the U.N. met in emer-
> gency session. The United States proposed a
> resolution condemning the actions of North
> Korean forces and calling for immediate cessa-
> tion of hostilities and the withdrawal of North
> Korean troops to the thirty-eight parallel. The
> resolution requested that the United Nations'
> temporary commission on Korea communicate
> its full considered recommendations on the situ-
> ation at once and called on every member to
> render every assistance to the United Nations
> in the execution of the resolution and to re-
> frain from giving assistance to the North Kore-
> ans.
>
> President Harry Truman interpreted the U.N.
> action as an authorization to assist the South
> Koreans militarily.... As the fighting contin-
> ued, with the United States providing most of
> the men and material, it became apparent the
> politicians in Washington and the U.N. were
> committed to a no-win policy.... We should
> have taken all of Korea and reunited this di-
> vided country. The politicians, fearful of pro-
> voking a full-scale conflict with the Red Chi-
> nese and Russia, refused to let [General]
> MacArthur pursue victory.[21]

Carroll Quigley, who may be best known as one of
Bill Clinton's professors, saw the situation differently.
He praised Democratic Pres. Harry Truman and the
U.N. for their handling of the situation. To Quigley,
the issue seemed to be as much safeguarding the vi-
ability of the U.N. as it was protecting South Korea.
He wrote:

> For forty-eight hours after the Korean attack,

the world hesitated, awaiting America's reaction. On June 26, 1950, the fifth birthday of the United Nations, many feared a "Munich," leading to the collapse of the whole United Nations security system at its first major challenge. Truman's reaction, however, was decisive. He immediately committed American air and sea forces in the area south of [the] 38 [parallel], and demanded a UN condemnation of the aggression. Thus, for the first time in history, a world organization voted to use collective force to stop armed aggression. This was possible because the North Korean attack occurred at a time when the Soviet delegation was absent from the United Nations Security Council, boycotting it in protest at the presence of the delegation from Nationalist China. Accordingly, the much-used Soviet veto was unavailable.[22]

The convenient absence of the Soviets enabled the United States to work with the U.N. against the North Korean Communists. But, when the Korean armistice was signed on 26 July 1953, Republican President Eisenhower joined in the accolades for the world body, saying, "We have seen the United Nations meet the challenge of aggression, not with pathetic words or protest but with deeds of decisive action."[23]

But, history has shown it was not decisive in the long run. The Communists remained in control of North Korea, while their patrons in Communist China and the Soviet Union mapped plans to spread communism to other countries. Meanwhile, a crisis emerged over the North Korean nuclear weapons program in 1994, causing military tensions on the Korean peninsula to rise to the point where another Korean War was being forecast.

Not surprisingly, the Clinton administration con-

sidered the U.N. option, threatening U.N. economic
sanctions against the Communists if they didn't abandon their nuclear program. In effect, however, the
administration was admitting that the U.N. had already demonstrated its ineffectiveness. The North
Koreans, after all, had been signatories to the Nuclear
Non-Proliferation Treaty, requiring regular inspections
by the U.N.-affiliated International Atomic Energy
Agency (IAEA). When it didn't serve their interests,
the Communists simply announced they would no
longer accept IAEA inspectors.

But, U.N. economic sanctions against North Korea didn't turn out to be necessary. Once again,
through the intervention of former Pres. Jimmy Carter,
who negotiated with the North Koreans, a compromise was reached. The Communists promised to give
up their nuclear weapons capability in exchange for
$4 billion in economic, financial, and political conces-
sions. Critics continue to contend that the North
Koreans cannot be trusted to live up to the agreement
and that key elements of it are unverifiable. In any
case, it will have no impact whatsoever on the North
Korean chemical/biological weapons program.

For its part, the United States is implementing the
agreement, and the North Koreans are said to antici-
pate diplomatic recognition by the United States, an
end to the U.S. trade embargo, and pressure by the
United States on South Korea to expand trade relations with the Communist North. There is even talk of
the prospective unification of the North with the South,
which the Communists had attempted through military means. Such talk alarms analyst Christopher Story,
who cautions,

> when the North is merged with the South, it
> will be the South which is transformed to the
> greatest extent. Northern cadres will infiltrate

the structures of the South, and the Korean miracle will suddenly take on a distinctly "socialist" hue.[24]

If the North reneges on the agreement, it is likely that the Clinton administration would, once again, go the U.N. route, seeking the implementation of economic sanctions. The administration seems determined to avoid either (1) unilateral U.S. action, such as a military strike, or (2) immediate development of a missile defense protecting the American people and our troops and allies overseas from missile attack. If the North doesn't renege on the agreement, the real prospect remains of North-South unification on Communist terms—something that Americans had died, under U.N. auspices, to prevent.

Meanwhile, the U.S. forces in Korea still remain under U.N. command. Indeed, the American people were reminded of this fact in December 1994, when the body of David Hilemon, the U.S. serviceman who was killed when the North Koreans shot down his unarmed U.S. reconnaissance helicopter, was returned by the Communists. The body was provided to a U.N. honor guard and carried in a coffin draped with a blue U.N. flag.[25]

Despite the no-win nature of the Korean War, Republican administrations continued a policy of cooperating, more or less, with the U.N. over the years. A different policy was attempted during the Reagan administration. In a Heritage Foundation report, Alan L. Keyes, former assistant secretary of state for International Organization Affairs, described how the Reagan administration handled the U.N., in contrast to how it was handled by previous administrations, especially that of Democratic Pres. Jimmy Carter:

A succession of U.S. Administrations have considered the U.N. as only marginally relevant to

key U.S. political and diplomatic interests, and
have used it primarily for political appeasement
of developing countries. This was especially the
case in the Carter Administration, when U.S.
delegates openly sympathized with the extreme
political and economic demands of the most
radical developing countries and "liberation
movements."

The Reagan Administration, by contrast, has
moved the U.N. up in priority, significantly
changing U.S. policy toward the U.N.. Although
the U.N. as an institution still is reflexively
hostile to U.S. values and interests, the U.S. at
the very least has made it clear that there are
limits to its patience, and that continued U.S.
support for, or even membership in, U.N. institutions cannot be taken for granted.[26]

Keyes emphasized the work of Jeane Kirkpatrick,
who served as U.S. ambassador to the U.N. from 1981
to 1985 and quit appeasing Third World nations and
strongly defended U.S. interests.

The Soviets despised Kirkpatrick, so much so that
a book on Soviet intelligence activities, *Washington
Station: My Life as a KGB Spy*, reveals that the Communists tried to smear her in a disinformation campaign.
According to former government official Herbert
Romerstein, who reviewed the book for *Human Events*
newspaper, the effort was designed to link Kirkpatrick
with the then-white minority government of South
Africa:

In 1982, the KGB launched "Operation Golf,"
designed to discredit the U.S. Ambassador to
the U.N., Jeane Kirkpatrick. Her U.N. speeches
had become a major thorn in the Soviets' side
by exposing their aggression and lies. "Operation Golf" was a forged letter ostensibly from

a South African embassy official to Ambassador Kirkpatrick, supposedly enclosing a birthday gift for her.[27]

Despite Kirkpatrick's best efforts, however, the U.N. remained mostly a large bureaucracy hostile to U.S. interests. Nothing demonstrates this fact more clearly than how the Heritage Foundation, a prominent conservative think tank, treated the world body. Heritage had also worked to change the organization through a United Nations Assessment Project, promoting needed reforms in the U.N. In fact, the project played a significant role in the U.S. withdrawal from the corrupt and anti-American UNESCO.[28]

However, a 1987 Heritage report by analyst Thomas E. L. Dewey urged the Democratic Congress to "freeze or reduce the U.S. contribution to the U.N." because the Reagan administration was not seen to be acting decisively enough.[29] Of course, the Democratic Congress also failed to implement the necessary reforms and, consequently, a 1989 Heritage study showed the U.N. was still up to its old tricks, with member nations of the U.N. voting in favor of U.S. positions only 17 percent of the time and with the Soviets 95 percent of the time.[30]

The circumstances, in other words, seemed ideal during the Bush administration for a renewed conservative push for U.S. withdrawal from the U.N. This was destined to change in 1990 when President Bush, urged on by his advisers, seized an opportunity to "revitalize" the U.N. by using the world body to mobilize the nations of the world against Iraq's invasion of Kuwait, which threatened America's oil supply.

At first, Bush, a former U.S. ambassador to the U.N., was skeptical that the United Nations would be of any use in backing a policy of aggressive action, even a blockade against Iraq. But, as Bob Woodward recounts in his book, *The Commanders,* Bush was talked into using the U.N.:

> The United Nations, which already had approved economic sanctions against Iraq, was now considering a resolution approving a blockade. The immediate question was whether to wait for the U.N., or go ahead unilaterally and board Iraqi ships. The Navy had stopped some Iraqi vessels, but had not yet boarded any.
>
> [Secretary of Defense Richard] Cheney could see that it was a huge decision for the President. Bush was clearly eager to assert the right of the United States to act by itself and wanted to demonstrate some muscle.... Nonetheless, Cheney recommended that the President not rush to board ships, but wait for the United Nations.
>
> [Chairman of the Joint Chiefs General Colin] Powell pointed out that shooting up a ship for a short-term gain would not be worth it.... From Wyoming, [Secretary of State James] Baker had made it clear that was his view also.
>
> Bush was skeptical the U.N. would come through. When he was U.N. ambassador in 1971–72, the Soviets had blocked everything the United States tried to do. But this was a new era. He decided he would wait for a ruling from the U.N. Security Council.[31]

The "new era" referred to perceived changes taking place in the Soviet Communist system. When the U.N. subsequently voted to enforce the trade embargo, Woodward wrote:

> It was the first time in the U.N.'s 45-year history that individual countries outside an umbrella U.N. command were authorized to en-

force an international blockade, an extraordinary diplomatic victory for the administration.[32]

This victory convinced the Bush administration to go further. The next step came when the U.N. Security Council met to vote on an authorization to use force to expel Iraq from Kuwait. There was a parallel with the Korea situation. "If it passed," Woodward wrote, "the resolution would be the broadest authority for war it had granted since Korea in 1950."[33] Any one of the five permanent members of the Security Council—the United States, China, Great Britain, France, or the Soviet Union—could have vetoed the resolution.

The Soviets were critical. They counted the Iraqi regime among their client states, had thousands of military advisers inside the country, and had supplied Iraqi forces with military equipment, including possibly chemical or biological weapons. Amazingly, they joined with the United States after a period of negotiation with Secretary of State James Baker. Woodward wrote, "The Soviets were the big question mark. From the beginning of the crisis, Gorbachev had opposed the possibility of military force, but he had finally come around."[34]

With Soviet backing, a resolution passed the Security Council endorsing the use of all necessary means to expel Iraq from Kuwait. But, then came the issue of whether the U.S. Congress—charged by the Constitution with the power to declare war—would approve such action. For the administration, there was some debate whether to even ask for approval from Congress. During a White House meeting on the subject, Deputy Attorney General William P. Barr argued that the president could act on his own, without Congress, as long as he had U.N. approval. Barr argued that

the situation most closely resembling the current crisis was the Korean War, when Truman acted without Congress under a United Nations resolution somewhat similar to the current one.[35]

In other words, the U.N. had become a substitute for America's elected representatives. Eventually, however, the Congress was consulted and a resolution similar in wording to that of the U.N. passed by 52 to 47 in the Senate and 250 to 183 in the House.

With U.N. backing, the United States and its allies launched an air war in 1991 that devastated Iraq. A land offensive was equally devastating. Saddam's forces were expelled from Kuwait in what was called the 100-hour War. The fact that total victory had not been achieved—that Iraqi ruler Saddam Hussein remained in power and that elements of the Iraqi Army were preserved—was played down. Gen. H. Norman Schwartzkopf, commander of allied forces in the Gulf, and General Powell became celebrated and admired U.S. military leaders, and President Bush's popularity soared.

For other reasons, mostly having to do with economic issues, Bush lost the presidency in 1992 to Bill Clinton, who would have no doubts whatsoever about relying on the U.N. In any case, the issue of what the United States had really accomplished in the Persian Gulf War soon emerged when, during a subsequent triumphant visit to Kuwait as ex-president, Bush became the target of an assassination attempt by agents of Iraq. Clinton, citing Article 51 of the U.N. Charter, retaliated by authorizing an American attack on Iraqi intelligence facilities.

But, that wasn't to be the only response Clinton would have to make to continuing Iraqi provocations. In October 1994, Iraq moved thousands of troops and tanks back toward the Kuwaiti border, in what appeared to be a replay of events preceding the Persian

Gulf War. Clinton responded by dispatching thirty-six thousand U.S. troops back to Kuwait, many of them Persian Gulf War veterans, forcing Iraq to back down.

This strange turn of events led the *New York Times* to run a story headlined, "How Iraq Escaped to Threaten Kuwait Again," adapted from the book titled *The Generals' War.* In response to questions from the authors, Michael R. Gordon and Bernard E. Trainor, former President Bush tried to explain his decision to end the war at one hundred hours, rather than pursue Iraqi forces all the way to Baghdad, the Iraqi capital: "The coalition was agreed on driving the Iraqis from Kuwait, not on carrying the conflict into Iraq or destroying Iraqi forces."[36]

The ex-president was referring, of course, to the U.N. mandates under which the coalition forces were operating. General Schwartzkopf made essentially the same point in his book:

> We had no less than nine United Nations resolutions authorizing our actions, and we had the support of virtually the entire world. But that support was for us to kick Iraq out of Kuwait, not to capture Baghdad.[37]

However, he went on to say it was advisable not to capture Baghdad because the United States would have become an occupying power and would have been responsible for rebuilding Iraq's economy and social structure. He said that would have meant that "we, not the United Nations, would be bearing the costs of that occupation." Schwartzkopf added, "This is a burden I am sure the beleaguered American taxpayer would not have been happy to take on."[38]

Moreover, Schwartzkopf wrote favorably of the U.N. and the need for international backing for U.S. military actions. Countering those who maintain the United States lost the Vietnam War primarily because of a failure of political will in Washington, Schwartzkopf argued:

> If we look back to the Vietnam War we should recognize that one of the reasons we lost world support for our actions was that we had no internationally recognized legitimacy for our intervention in Vietnam.[39]

It is surprising that Schwartzkopf places such value on what the international community thinks. It suggests that General Shalikashvili, who endorsed making NATO a partner in U.N. operations, is not alone among top U.S. military commanders in thinking that the U.N. provides needed "legitimacy" to United States and allied military operations.

In the case of Iraq, however, the legitimacy did not produce the advantages Schwartzkopf thought they would. Even without an occupation of Baghdad, the United States still pays a significant share of the cost for U.N. operations in the area and is still involved militarily. Indeed, the stakes involved were dramatized when twenty-six people, including fifteen Americans, died in an April 1994 "friendly fire" incident in the skies over Iraq, as two U.S. helicopters were downed by American jets which mistook them for enemy aircraft. When Vice President Gore delivered the eulogy for the dead Americans, he extended "condolences to the families of those who died in the service of the United Nations," rather than highlight their U.S. military service. Columnist Robert Novak asked, "Did that mean the coffins containing 14 members of the U.S. military and one State Department official ought to be draped in the blue-and-white U.N. flag?"[40]

As in Korea, the involvement of the U.N. is the key to understanding why total victory was not achieved. The war was not run by the U.N., but the involvement of this body inhibited the kind of decisive military action that would have destroyed the enemy.

Schwartzkopf is not alone in failing to understand this. General Powell, who is talked about as a Republican presidential or vice presidential candidate in 1996, will have to explain why, according to the Woodward book, he also insisted on relying on the U.N. in the Persian Gulf War.

Howard Means, author of a biography of Powell, noted that the outcome of the war is a critical issue:

> Although the United Nations mandate under which the Allied force was operating never called for the ouster of Saddam Hussein, his continued presence in Baghdad does remain the problem in any evaluation of the success of Operation Desert Storm.[41]

The Means book, published in 1992, said Powell's position was that, even though Saddam survived the war, he survived "in such a diminished state that he is a threat only to his own people."[42] Powell told CNN in a 1992 interview:

> I don't know how much longer he's [Saddam] going to stay in power. I think the world would be better off and, most important, the people of Iraq would be better off were he to leave power. He is not in as strong a position as some of these one-year retrospectives would have you believe. He no longer has an army that's capable of generating an offense that would threaten its neighbors. . . . He is an irritation as far as I'm concerned. He is not causing me a great deal of stress.[43]

By contrast, even before Saddam's forces returned to threaten Kuwait, retired Col. David Hackworth declared in a 20 January 1992 column for *Newsweek* that Schwartzkopf and Powell, the key generals in "The Generals' War," should have insisted on total victory for the sake of their men. Hackworth said they had the obligation to say to President Bush what Gen. George Marshall had said to President Franklin Roosevelt at the outbreak of World War II—"that the goal had to be unconditional surrender and the destruction of enemy military capability." If Bush had gotten such advice, Hackworth said, "The President could then have told the United Nations that only the elimination of Saddam Hussein would justify Allied soldiers climbing out of their foxholes."[44]

As a result, the Persian Gulf War "victory" today seems hollow. In fact, an estimate published by *Jane's Intelligence Review* in January 1995, revealed that Iraq's military had reconstituted "a considerable portion of its pre-Desert Storm combat power," remained a "potent threat" to Kuwait and Saudi Arabia, and could soon emerge as a "dominant force in the Gulf." The Iraqi Armed Forces were described as 400,000-strong, down from 1 million at the time of the Persian Gulf War, but still more than twice that of Saudi Arabia.[45]

Not only did Saddam reemerge to threaten Kuwait again, but some analysts said evidence pointed to an Iraqi role in the 1993 bombing of the World Trade Center in New York. Moreover, *New York Times* columnist William Safire reported that, despite the presence of U.N. "inspectors" in the country, Iraq's biological weapons program was back on track, headed by a character known as "Dr. Germs." Arguing for continuation of the embargo against Iraq, Safire said, "If the world lets heavy money flow to Baghdad while Saddam rules, at least one weapon of mass destruction will soon be in the hands of a proven killer. He would delight in being the first to use it."[46] Ironically, Safire seemed oblivious to evidence that Saddam had already used such weapons in the Persian Gulf War, contributing to the Persian Gulf War syndrome that was making tens of thousands of Gulf War veterans sick.

Indeed, although all the evidence is not in, there is no doubt that the United States suffered far more casualties than commonly believed in the Persian Gulf War, and that Gulf War Syndrome may be linked to the use of Iraqi chemical or biological weapons supplied by Moscow and tested on our troops. Estimates of the number of Persian Gulf War vets suffering from these health ailments, including chronic fatigue, aching joints, and memory loss, range as high as fifty thousand. Almost seven hundred thousand served in the Gulf during the war.

Under these circumstances, if the Republicans nominate General Powell for a place on their ticket in 1996, they will have fielded a candidate whose reputation will be tainted by his serious misjudgments in the Persian Gulf War. Once seen as the most popular man in America, Powell could instead come to be viewed as a liability. The Republicans cannot afford to make this mistake at a time when Clinton's pro-U.N. policy needs to be directly challenged.

Notes

1. "America's Place in the Post Cold War World," Times Mirror Center for the People and the Press, Washington, D.C. (2 November 1993): 26–27.

2. *Contract with America: The Bold Plan by Rep. Newt Gingrich, Rep. Dick Armey and the House Republicans To Change the Nation* (New York: Times Books, 1994), 91.

3. Ibid., 101.

4. Jeane Kirkpatrick, "Dole Would Limit U.N. Role in U.S. Foreign Policy," *Human Events* (27 January 1995): 20.

5. Lee A. Casey and David B. Rivkin, Jr., "Congress, the President and the U.N.," *Washington Times* (30 January 1995).

6. Ibid.

7. See "A U.N. Army: Unwise, Unsafe and Unnecessary," by Thomas P. Sheehy, policy analyst, the Heritage Foundation, 16 September 1995.

8. Ibid., *Contract with America*, 105.

9. William Matthews, "Perry Asks OK to Bust Budgets," *Army Times* (3 April 1995): 15.

10. Sen. Bob Dole, testimony, Senate Committee on Foreign Relations, 21 March 1995.

11. R. Jeffrey Smith and Julia Preston, "Secret U.S. Papers Left in Somalia," *Washington Post* (12 March 1995): 1.

12. *Freedom From War. The United States Program for General and Complete Disarmament in a Peaceful World*, Department of State publication 7277, released September 1961.

13. Ibid., 3.

14. Eric Cox, letter to the editor, *New York Times*, sec. 1, col. 4 (25 March 1989): 26.

15. Sandford Lee Persons, letter to the editor, *New York Times*, 20 November 1983, sec. 4, 20.

16. Barbara Crossette, "White House Backs Away From Plan to Rejoin UNESCO," *New York Times* (1 January 1995): 12.

17. *Cato Handbook for the 104th Congress*, Cato Institute, 1995, 285.

18. See Kevin Phillips, "Special Issue: Washington and the Republican Revolution: 1995-96 Prospects," *American Political Report* (30 December 1994).

19. "The U.S. and the UN: Myths and Realities," remarks by Lee Edwards, 24 October 1994.

20. Barry M. Goldwater, *Why Not Victory?: A Fresh Look at American Foreign Policy* (New York: McGraw-Hill, 1962), 142.

21. Barry M. Goldwater, *With No Apologies* (New York: William Morrow and Company Inc., 1979), 47–48.

22. Carroll Quigley, *Tragedy and Hope: A History of the World in Our Times* (New York: The Macmillan Company, 1966), 972.

23. See Chesly Manly, *The UN Record, Ten Fateful Years for America* (Chicago: Henry Regnery Company, 1955), 54.

24. *International Currency Review*, vol. 22, nos. 3–4 (Autumn 1994): 81.

25. See the *Times*, 23 December 1994, and the *Commercial Appeal* (Memphis), 22 December 1994.

26. Alan L. Keyes, "The United Nations," *Mandate for Leadership III, Policy Strategies for the 1990s*, edited by Charles Heatherly and Burton Yale Pines, (The Heritage Foundation: Washington, D.C., 1989): 654.

27. Herbert Romerstein, "New Book Exposes Journalist and Caterite as KGB Tools," *Human Events* (13 January 1995): 12.

28. Edwin J. Feulner, president, the Heritage Foundation, "Dear Fellow American," letter, undated.

29. Thomas E.L. Dewey, "The Charade of United Nations Reform," Backgrounder, the Heritage Foundation (21 December 1987).

30. Mark A. Franz, director, United Nations Assessment Project, "Report on Voting Practices at the United Nations, 44th General Assembly," the Heritage Foundation, (20 July 1990).

31. Bob Woodward, *The Commanders* (New York: Simon and Schuster, 1991), 284.

32. Ibid., 285.

33. Ibid., 333.

34. Ibid.

35. Ibid., 357.

36. Michael R. Gordon and Bernard E. Trainor, "How Iraq Escaped to Threaten Kuwait Again," *New York Times* (23 October 1994): 10.

37. Gen. H. Norman Schwartzkopf, *It Doesn't Take a Hero* (New York: Bantam Books, October 1993), 581.

38. Ibid., 580–581.

39. Ibid., 581.

40. Robert Novak, "Clinton Ties U.S. Hands in UN Role," *Chicago Sun-Times* (25 April 1994).

41. Howard Means, *Colin Powell: A Biography* (New York: Ballantine Books, 1992), 272.

42. Ibid.

43. Ibid.

44. Ibid.

45. Dr. Andrew Rathmell, "Iraq's Military—Waiting For Change," Jane's Information Group, vol. 7, no 2.

46. William Safire, "Iraq's Threat: Biological Warfare," *New York Times* (16 February 1995).

The U.N.

4

Corruption

If there is anything holding the U.N. back from its dream of world government, it could very well be massive corruption and financial problems that threaten to result in the organization's literal collapse. In comparison to the U.N., the Democratic-controlled U.S. Congress—with its check-bouncing schemes, sex scandals, high salaries, and inflated pensions—looked squeaky clean. The difference is that the American people voted most of the corrupt Democrats out of Congress while U.N. bureaucrats continue enjoying the high life at our expense.

In an extraordinary admission, Cedric Thornberry, former U.N. director of administration, disclosed that the organization nearly went bankrupt on two occasions in the 1980s. He blamed this on governments failing to contribute funds, an apparent slap in the face of the United States, by far the biggest "contributor."[1]

But, the reason the Reagan administration stopped paying its full U.N. dues in 1986 was because of the U.N.'s inability to do anything about budgetary waste and financial mismanagement.[2] The Reagan administration was so discouraged by a failure to eradicate

waste, fraud, and abuse in the world body that it figured the only way to prompt reform was to withhold
funds.

How much has changed over the years? President
Clinton's ambassador to the U.N., Madeleine Albright,
admitted to Congress last year that

> press reports exaggerate but I cannot justify to
> the taxpayers of my country some of the per-
> sonnel arrangements, sweetheart pension deals,
> lack of accountability, duplication of effort and
> lack of attention to the bottom line that we so
> often see around here—that is, the U.N.'s poor
> management is the Achilles heel of the United
> Nations.[3]

Amid great fanfare, the U.N. announced in the
fall of 1993 that an Egyptian accountant was being
named to the position of U.N. assistant secretary general for inspections and investigations. His job was
supposed to be to root out rampant corruption. But,
the announcement was really designed to take some
of the edge off two dramatic investigative reports into
waste, fraud, and abuse in the U.N.

The *Sunday Times* of London had already carried
a major exposé noting that "senior U.N. officials continue to enjoy generous benefits, perks, and job-for-
life expectations that would never be tolerated outside." Calling the U.N. "a bureaucracy run wild," the
paper said that "internal audit reports reveal an alarming pattern of abuse, mismanagement and greed which
has become endemic in the organization." Some of
the worst fraud, the paper said, was "in programs
designed to help the most disadvantaged people."[4]

It was difficult, the paper indicated, to even get a
handle on the size and scope of the problem:

> The UN has more than 50 agencies and 100
> committees and special ad hoc bodies, known

by an alphabet soup of acronyms that few
outsiders comprehend. . . . The institutions are
scattered across the world, sometimes, it seems,
for no other purpose than to give UN member
states a UN agency of their own. . . .

The titles of the UN's latest publications list
include: "The science and praxis of complex-
ity; the findings of a UN sponsored symposium
which explored the subject of interdisciplinary
and real life complexities in the social sciences."

Another paper, entitled "Imperialism: the Permanent Stage of Capitalism," contends that
imperialism—not hunger or disease—is the most
important problem of the world. "This work
undertakes a critique of established liberal,
radical and Marxist approaches to the subject,"
it announces.

Earlier this year, the UN Department for Human Rights issued its latest Human Rights Year-
book—for 1986. Production delays meant it was
seven years too late.[5]

Another major investigative treatment of the U.N.
was in the works when the U.N. created its office of
"high-level corruption investigator." This story, which
aired on 19 September, opened with correspondent
Mike Wallace of the popular CBS "60 Minutes" program saying:

When the UN General Assembly reconvenes
Tuesday in New York, what will not be on the
public agenda is waste and fraud at the UN.
But privately, more than a few UN diplomats
have acknowledged to us that waste and fraud
there is increasingly on their minds.[6]

Wallace said that "many in a position to know
charge that disturbing amounts" of money from the

U.N. budget "are disappearing due to mismanagement or corruption." Charles Lichenstein, a U.S. representative to the U.N. from 1981 to 1984, told Wallace that he believed that "probably hundreds of millions" of dollars were being wasted by the U.N. every year. Referring to the U.N.'s growing involvement in peacekeeping, Wallace said, "So while we look to the UN as the world's policeman, its ability to police itself is quite another matter."

Sen. Larry Pressler, who sponsored legislation forcing the U.N. to create a post of inspector general, told Wallace that while he likes and supports the U.N. as "the best hope in the world today," he believes that the American taxpayers will stop supporting the world body when they find out about some of the "outrageous" things taking place there.

In true "60 Minutes"-style, Wallace engaged in some eye-opening exchanges with Melissa Wells, an American who serves as U.N. undersecretary in charge of management. Concerning a U.N. operation in Cambodia, which had been hailed as a success, Wallace referred to 1) millions spent on a water purification system that didn't work, 2) U.N. officials accused of incompetence and lack of integrity who weren't fired, and 3) U.N. investigations of fraud that "have been dragging on now for more than nine full months." Wells responded, "I'd be the first to say that we have a lot to learn. And we are learning it. And we've made some mistakes, some bad mistakes." Asked when was the last time that a U.N. official was prosecuted for theft, corruption, or breaking the law, Wells said, "I'd have to look it up."

Like the *Sunday Times*, Wallace focused on what he called "the U.N.'s vast underground printing establishment, which grinds out almost a billion pages of documents each year," many of them completely out of date, worthless, or ideologically driven. Holding up a copy of a U.N. document containing the official records of the U.N. Security Council for 16 August 1984, Wallace told Wells it had been published in 1993, nine years later. After being pressed, Wells conceded, "Well, that seems rather lengthy, yes."

Another revealing exchange took place between Wallace and Marco Vianello-Chiodo, who heads the U.N.'s largest department, public information. Wallace said Vianello-Chiodo said he would gladly cut seven hundred of the one thousand people who presently work for him and invest the savings in new programs and automation. But, Vianello-Chiodo said he couldn't do that.

> Wallace: I understand you are under orders from the secretary-general not to fire people.
>
> Mr. Marco Vianello-Chiodo: Yes.
>
> Wallace: Because?
>
> Mr. Vianello-Chiodo: I don't think the system allows that. You know, this is 48 years of not firing anybody, so it would be very difficult to start now.[7]

This is the same Boutros-Ghali who, after being chosen as U.N. secretary general, reportedly visited the U.N. headquarters and declared, "There are thousands of staff. Half of them do no work."[8] But, the U.N. information office was not unique. Lichenstein said former U.N. Secretary General Xavier Perez de Cuellar and his staff prepared a list of some one hundred U.N. programs that were either duplicative or out of date and needed to be closed down. What happened? Lichenstein said, "Nothing."

One such program is the U.N. Trusteeship Council, one of the six major organs of the U.N., established back in 1946 to oversee the governing of some eleven territories around the world. Today, Wallace

noted, there is just one territory left, Palau, with fifteen thousand citizens. And yet, the U.N. Trusteeship
Council keeps meeting to discuss what Lichenstein
laughingly called "urgent issues."

One of the most embarrassing U.N. management
fiascoes, cited by Wallace on "60 Minutes," occurred
in the early 1980s when an official at the Office of the
U.N. High Commissioner for Refugees (UNHCR) was
accused of running a prostitution ring out of his U.N.
office. Rather than being fired, he was transferred to
a UNHCR office in Africa, where more than $2 mil-
lion worth of food, goods, and equipment was misap-
propriated. His friends in the U.N. bureaucracy protected him and even threatened the life of a U.S.
official investigating his activities. He was eventually
transferred to head the UNHCR office in Djibouti,
the center of the refugee relief efforts for both Somalia and Ethiopia. There, massive shipments of food aid
sent to his office disappeared before they could be
distributed to starving refugees, and he was charged
with misappropriating almost $700,000, including seven
payments worth $346,000 that went to fictitious com-
panies. This caused the unnecessary starvation deaths
of thousands of Ethiopians and Somalians.[9] Yet,
Wallace noted, "he was still able to collect his full
pension and leave, and the U.N. never prosecuted
him."

A great deal of money is spent on conference
centers and conferences. Wallace noted that a U.N.
center in Ethiopia, one of the most poverty-stricken
areas in the world, alone cost $100 million.

It pays well for U.N. bureaucrats to say they're
against poverty. The March 1995 U.N. World Summit
for Social Development described itself as "a global
attack on extreme poverty, unemployment and all
forms of discrimination and intolerance." However,
the summit itself was estimated to cost $30 million.

One world leader, President Bakili Muluzi of Malawi, one of the poorest countries in the world, decided to cancel his trip to the summit to save money. "A trip to Copenhagen would have cost $200,000 for him and his delegation, and Muluzi said he would rather see the money go toward alleviating poverty at home," the *Washington Post* reported. But, conference delegates, many of them with "fat expense accounts," jammed fancy hotels and restaurants and did not seem to mind paying "some of the most exorbitant prices in the world," the paper said, while a "lavish banquet" was held for the summit's most distinguished guests.[10]

But no one, not even the main organizer of the world summit, Juan Somavia of Chile, could articulate exactly what it would accomplish. "We've been going at the problem of poverty for so long, we should be able to make a clear decision to eliminate the worst forms of poverty," Somavia said in an interview. *Washington Post* reporter Julia Preston commented, "But decades of U.N. pronouncements in favor of this unimpeachable goal have not brought financially strapped governments closer to reaching it."[11]

Eradicating poverty is a favorite goal of U.N. conferences, including the 1992 Earth Summit, officially called the U.N. Conference on Environment and Development. Eliminating poverty was also an objective of the Cairo population conference in September 1994 (costing $5 million), a women's conference in Beijing, China, scheduled for September 1995 (at a projected cost of $5.5 million), and the U.N. fiftieth anniversary commemoration (cost unknown).

But, a full list of recent U.N. conferences would have to include the World Summit for Children, the World Conference on Human Rights, the Global Conference on the Sustainable Development of Small Island Developing States, and the World Conference on Natural Disaster Reduction.

The liberal *Washington Post* even acted perplexed by the holding of the world summit, saying that "the most ardent advocates of the United Nations may wonder what the organization is doing running yet another mass conference, this one designed to assemble heads of state, on a 'soft' global topic." The paper said that the apparent purpose, to tackle the world's problems through "collective international efforts," ignored the fact that there is already a series of international institutions in place to do just that.[12]

The cost of the U.N.'s fiftieth anniversary celebration could far surpass what has been spent on any of these conferences. The focus of much of the activity was a scheduled "special commemorative meeting" of the U.N. General Assembly in October of 1995, to which heads of state or government were invited.

By the summer of 1994, however, the U.N. was already gearing up, publishing a "Newsletter of the 50th Anniversary of the United Nations" that announced "dozens" of "UN50" conferences and symposia during 1995 and even publication of a "UN50 1995 Calender."

At least eighty-four countries, including the United States, were reported to have established "National Committees" to organize pro-U.N. events. In the United States, the activities were scheduled to include the traditional U.N. Week in October, featuring participation by schools and communities. An "education packet" was supposed to be ready by the spring, enabling students at "various grade levels" to help celebrate the U.N.'s anniversary. These materials were going to include the "Children's History of the United Nations," the documentary series "Under the Blue Flag," and a film "Global Youth." Not too bad for an organization that almost went bankrupt.

However, the propaganda barrage in favor of the U.N. was facing one big problem—continuing reports of serious financial misconduct at the organization. Even the *Washington Post's* U.N. correspondent, Julia Preston, considered sympathetic to the world body, was reporting that incompetence and unaccountability were still serious problems:

> U.N. employees get raises and promotions regardless of the work they actually do. Two separate U.N. agencies run virtually identical programs on behalf of women, but politics has blocked officials from ending the costly duplication. A new, million-dollar security system at U.N. headquarters in New York did not work and had to be scrapped—and administrators cannot even say with certainty who approved the project.[13]

The U.N.'s inspector general, a German named Karl Theodore Paschke, came under fire. Preston admitted he "has been slow off the mark" and that, in the five months since he started in November 1994, he had issued only one public report—about a $4 million theft in the U.N. mission in Somalia which was investigated before he took office. Paschke's complaint, a typical one at the U.N., was that he needed more money and staff to get the job done.[14] One key problem with the U.N.—which will also apply to their promised world government—is the sheer complexity of the operation. When it was founded in 1945, it employed just fifteen hundred people. According to the U.N. Information Center in Washington, D.C., the organization today employs some fifty-two thousand people worldwide, forty-eight hundred of them in New York.

An official diagram of the U.N. "system" shows that there are six "central organs" under which everything else falls. These organs are the International Court of Justice, the General Assembly, the Economic and Social Council, the Security Council, the Secretariat, and the Trusteeship Council.

Under the General Assembly are an unspecified number of "main and other sessional committees," "standing committees and ad hoc bodies," and "other subsidiary organs and related bodies." Also under the control of the General Assembly is the International Atomic Energy Agency (IAEA), the group that was supposed to prevent North Korea from developing a nuclear weapons capability.

Under the province of the General Assembly and the Economic and Social Council are thirteen special U.N. agencies, including the U.N. International Drug Control Program, the U.N. Population Fund, and the U.N. Development Program. Under the Economic and Social Council are nine "functional commissions" on issues like the status of women, five "regional commissions," and an unspecified number of "sessional and standing committees" and "expert, ad hoc and related bodies." Also under the Economic and Social Council are eighteen more agencies, including the U.N. Educational, Scientific and Cultural Organization, the World Health Organization, the World Bank Group of organizations, the International Monetary Fund, and the World Trade Organization.

Bodies under the Security Council include a "Military Staff Committee," various "standing committees and ad hoc bodies," and the assorted peacekeeping operations, numbering sixteen as of March 1995.[15]

Although it's not specifically identified on the official chart of the U.N. "system," the U.N. even has its own university, the United Nations University (UNU), which operates on the basis of an endowment fund worth $283 million and an annual budget of about $30 million. The UNU's educational program for 1994–95, covering the fiftieth anniversary of the world body, is titled "The United Nations System, Global Governance and Security."

But, figuring out how much money is spent on the U.N. can be just as frustrating as trying to find out where it goes. The U.N. Information Center reports that the 1994–95 U.N. "regular" budget is $2.6 billion, 25 percent of which is paid by the United States. But, this $2.6 billion figure does not include expenditures made by different U.N. funds and programs, which are covered by "voluntary contributions" from member states. For example, the U.N. Development Program had a separate $1.4 billion budget in 1993, with the United States "contributing" the largest amount, $125 million. The UNDP has seven thousand staff members in 131 countries.

U.N. peacekeeping is another category. The U.N. Information Center says the 1994 budget for U.N. peacekeeping was roughly $3 billion. The United States pays about 30 percent of the cost of peacekeeping, although this figure is scheduled to drop to 25 percent as of 1 January 1996. But, these "official" figures are highly misleading. Sen. Robert Dole says the United States has spent more than $10 billion on U.N. peacekeeping in the 1992–95 period, much of it money not appropriated by Congress for that purpose.

In a Ford Foundation report, *Renewing the United Nations System*, former U.N. officials Erskine Childers and Brian Urquhart estimate that the U.N. spends about $10.5 billion a year.[16] In a similar vein, the "60 Minutes" program put U.N. spending at $10 billion a year. But, these figures may not include the full costs of U.N. peacekeeping cited by Dole—money "contributed" by the United States to the U.N. outside of normal budgetary procedures.

A realistic estimate, therefore, is that the United States may be spending $5 billion a year on the U.N.

In any case, the United States contributes far more than any other nation. Japan contributes 12.5 percent,

Russia contributes 9.4 percent, Germany contributes 8.9 percent, and France contributes 6 percent of the U.N. general budget.[17] This means that "American taxpayers continue to underwrite a large portion of the United Nations' often wasteful and mismanaged (and sometimes anti-American) programs," as the Cato Institute put it.[18]

The sad fact, which figures to be largely overlooked during the U.N.'s fiftieth anniversary year, is that there is no legitimate hope that the "reforms" which have been promised for years will ever be seriously carried out. Reforms at the U.N. have historically been stonewalled and weakened by an army of thousands of U.N. bureaucrats who are fearful of losing their jobs. In true bureaucratic style, their only way out is to demand even more money. But, the billions already spent on the U.N. could pale in comparison to what U.N. bureaucrats think is required in the future to pay their salaries and pensions.

In preparation for the U.N. World Summit for Social Development in March of 1995, the U.N. Development Program issued a report urging a series of global taxes and cutbacks in military spending so that an additional $1.5 trillion in revenues could flow to a "revitalized" U.N. over the next five-year period. This would, of course, remove any incentive to eliminate waste, fraud, and abuse within the system.

Considering the U.N.'s poor track record in fighting corruption, it might be thought that there would be no chance whatsoever of generating these kinds of revenues. But, pro-U.N. groups, such as the corporate- and foundation-funded U.N. Association of the U.S., have found a unique way to keep the U.N. bureaucracy going and growing. They are peddling the argument that cuts in funding for the U.N. could hurt U.S. firms doing business with the world body. In 1993, they claim that U.S. firms benefited from $494 million worth of commercial transactions with the U.N. and have produced a book, *How To Do Business With the UN*, advising American companies on how they can get in on more of the business. Advancing another argument against U.N. cutbacks, the group insists that the U.N.'s New York headquarters generates $1 billion in business for the city's economy.

But, companies doing business with the U.N. do so at their own risk. When an Australian firm, Morris Catering, which supplied U.N. peacekeeping troops in Somalia with food, couldn't get $20 million it was owed by the U.N. and couldn't pay the $2 million it owed to its creditors inside Somalia, two employees of the company in Somalia were taken hostage as ransom. Company owner David Morris, who offered himself as security to win the release of the two employees, was then faced with physical mutilation, such as lopping off an ear or finger, if his company didn't pay up.[19]

The only faint hope of reforming the organization lies in this area of peacekeeping. Waste, fraud, and abuse were acceptable as long as the U.N. existed mainly as a propaganda forum for international bureaucrats. However, once the U.N. accelerated its involvement in military operations around the world, it occurred to some U.N. bureaucrats that a minimal level of competence was required. In other words, the U.N. had to be able to actually deploy and equip troops in the field.

There were already warning signs in this area. By July of 1993, the U.N. had launched its own investigation into irregularities in the awarding of contracts to supply U.N. peacekeeping forces. At one point, the U.N. withheld $20 million in payments to a Canadian charter aircraft company, Skylink Aviation, which transports U.N. troops and equipment around the world. Skylink threatened to ground all its aircraft if the U.N. did not pay up.[20]

The most devastating indictment of U.N. practices, especially in the peacekeeping field, came in a report issued in late 1994 by a group of experts. The timing of the report was revealing; it was issued during the Christmas holidays on 23 December. Catherine Toups of the *Washington Times*, got hold of it, noting:

> The United Nations has wasted millions of dollars because of shoddy, outdated procurement practices, an internal investigation . . . indicated.
>
> The announcement was among three highly controversial cases released on the day before Christmas Eve, when most reporters were gone and news consumption competes with Christmas activities.[21]

One of these controversial announcements, incidentally, involved the aforementioned Skylink. The U.N. disciplined four employees for misconduct and unprofessionalism in awarding contracts to the company.

It's understandable why U.N. bureaucrats didn't want the press to cover this announcement or the report on procurement practices. This devastating report, the result of an internal investigation conducted over the period of just two months, was a massive indictment of the U.N. procurement system used in the peacekeeping field. The authors said that, unless major reforms were forthcoming in U.N. operations, the U.N. itself could fold from the weight of sheer incompetence: "The very credibility of the United Nations stands or falls on whether it can project its presence where and when it is needed in an efficient and professional manner."[22]

In setting the stage for its indictment of U.N.
practices, the report described the rapid growth of
U.N. operations, including peacekeeping and humanitarian assistance, and flatly declared, "The United Nations capacity to implement and support such operations has lagged far behind this demand."[23]

How far behind? Incredibly, the study found that
the U.N. procurement process was "stuck in a time
warp," had not been improved over a period of more
than thirty years, and that the procurement area had
been considered "unimportant" by U.N. officials, an
area where "inexperienced, untrained or unwanted
staff are put."[24] The study said that the list of vendors,
or possible suppliers of needed equipment, was "out
of date, inaccurate and lacks the credibility and con-
fidence of the Member States as well as, of course, the
Buyers." It found that contracts made for the purchase of equipment did not even include a provision
giving the U.N. the right to take action against Vendors "who failed to perform." It added, "There is a
singular lack of any meaningful performance measur-
ing taking place, not just in the financial sense but
also, in terms of delivery dates, workload, lead times,
equipment reliability and the like."

The procurement experts said they found it "difficult" to understand how the peacekeeping operations had been able to continue for so long "without
producing performance data to justify its resource
requirements."

In a related matter, the peacekeeping troops themselves, most of them from Third World countries, are
coming under scrutiny. Allegations of pedophilia surfaced against members of the U.N. peacekeeping
operation in Mozambique, which was costing the U.N.
$210 million annually. Supposedly there on a humani-
tarian mission, some of the seven thousand or eight
thousand U.N. troops were accused by relief workers

of paying for sex with children twelve to fourteen years old. Behrooz Sadry, deputy special representative of the U.N. secretary-general in Mozambique, confirmed in early 1994 that in some cities prostitution "increased perceptibly" after U.N. troops arrived. He confirmed that the troops had hired prostitutes, some of them minors, and that some of the offenders had been sent home.[25]

There are those who admit that while the U.N. has its share of problems, some specialized U.N. agencies do good work. Yet, in March of 1995, one of the most admired U.N. agencies, the U.N. Children's Fund (UNICEF), was also mired in scandal, when its deputy director disclosed that seven employees in its Kenya office had been charged with fraud and other financial irregularities and that three others were put on suspension. The *Washington Times* reported that the irregularities included allegations of hiring prostitutes— a charge denied by the UNICEF office in New York— and that the financial fraud could involve as much as $10 million.

Another worthwhile U.N. agency, according to *Washington Post* reporter Julia Preston, is the fifty-four-nation U.S. Economic and Social Council (ECOSOC), which decides how U.N. agencies should spend more than $1 billion a year. Preston contends that it has become a positive force because "big bucks and big powers" helped streamline the operation.

However, Preston herself ignored a major embarrassment suffered by the ECOSOC when the United States and other member nations, including Russia and Cuba, voted in July 1993 to award special ECOSOC status to the International Lesbian and Gay Association (ILGA). ILGA had waged a ten-year effort to gain this coveted U.N. affiliation.

But, Peter LaBarbera, the investigative editor of the *Lamba Report on Homosexuality*, disclosed that

ILGA's members included pedophile groups such as the notorious North American Man-Boy Love Association (NAMBLA), whose members have been arrested on child abuse charges.

The disclosure created enormous public relations problems for the U.N. After all, the U.N. is supposed to be against the sexual abuse of children. In 1990, the U.N. Human Rights Commission had ordered an investigation of international child prostitution and child pornography rings, finding that they are "global . . . and much more extensive than is apparent at first glance."[26] Marlise Simons, a correspondent for the *New York Times*, reported the existence of "secretive, international networks of pedophiles who swap information on 'safe resorts,' specialized brothels and 'safe houses' and promote these in their fancy brochures and videotapes."[27] Significantly, Simons focused on Thailand, a country that is regularly advertised in U.S. homosexual magazines as a place for pedophiles to visit. A typical ad says, "Let your travel fantasies soar," and features a photograph of a teenage Thai boy.[28]

Simons described what happens to these children, whom she called the "littlest prostitutes":

> Abuse and disease are rampant. The harm to their bodies is easiest to record: cigarette burns, self-inflicted cuts, syphilis and gonorrhea, and increasingly, the virus that causes AIDS.[29]

The controversy sparked by LaBarbera's revelations about ILGA's pedophile ties prompted the U.S. Congress to pass a law requiring a cut-off of U.S. funds to the ECOSOC unless ILGA expelled its pedophile members. Eventually, under U.S. pressure, the ECOSOC suspended ILGA's membership because the organization failed to expel all the pedophiles.

The controversy demonstrated how haphazard and confusing U.N. decision making and operations fre-

quently are. The U.S. delegation claimed that it was
not aware of ILGA's pedophile ties when it voted to
give the group special U.N. status. If true, this raises
serious questions about the procedures in place, if
any, to evaluate members, policies, and other U.N.-
related activities.

To make matters worse, the same questions apply
to how the organization treats sex problems within its
own ranks.

When *Washington Times* reporter Catherine Toups
noted that the U.N. had released announcements about
several controversial cases on the day before Christmas Eve 1994, when virtually no reporter was paying
attention, she said that one of them involved partial
resolution of a sexual harassment case:

> Catherine Claxton, who has worked at the
> United Nations for eighteen years, was awarded
> ninety-four thousand dollars in an out-of-court
> settlement after she complained that her boss,
> Luis Maria Gomez, an Argentine, grabbed her
> and made sexual advances. She also was given
> $116,800 for legal fees and court costs.[30]

Ironically, Toups reported, the settlement included
damages not for the harassment itself, but for the
"prolonged and complex nature of the proceedings
that led to the resolution of her case."

The Gomez case symbolizes much of what is wrong
with the U.N. Though located in New York City, the
U.N. is considered to be on international territory
covered by diplomatic immunity. Because Gomez had
diplomatic immunity, no criminal charges were ever
filed against him.

As a U.N. employee, Claxton's first option was to
seek justice within the U.N. system. This resulted in
the "prolonged and complex" proceedings referred to
in the Toups dispatch. And, the history of the case is

important in evaluating how seriously the U.N. should expect to be taken when it holds conferences, such as the one in Beijing in 1995, on how to treat women better.

The Claxton case dates back to March 1988, when Claxton says that Gomez grabbed, kissed, and fondled her. A U.N. report on the incident, which was said to have occurred in Gomez's office, described what happened after Gomez began making sexual remarks to her.

> She decided she would leave, and when she stood up, he moved over to her. He grabbed her by the shoulders and upper arms and forced his tongue into her mouth. He moved his right hand to her buttock and pulled her against him and then moved that hand to her breast. At this stage she was able to pull free.[31]

Gomez had enjoyed a series of high positions in the U.N. and had friends in high places. He had served in the powerful position of U.N. comptroller, where he was in charge of U.N. financial practices. He had also served as the number two official at the U.N. Development Program. Gomez's lawyer, attorney Alan Dershowitz, denied the charges against his client and pointed out that there were no U.N. guidelines on sexual harassment when the incident was said to have taken place. Moreover, Claxton waited three and one-half years, until 1991, before filing a complaint with the U.N. Administrative Tribunal. However, her supporters said the filing was delayed because she had been too intimidated to make a formal protest and she reportedly told a co-worker about the incident the day after it happened. Other U.N. employees testified that they saw bruises on her shoulders.[32] Still other employees came forward to say that Gomez was known for making sexual comments and that he had requested sexual intercourse from some women in exchange for promotions in their jobs.[33]

The actions of Secretary General Boutros-Ghali in this case are also revealing. He took office in January 1992, after Claxton filed her complaint. He appointed an outside judge, Mella Carroll, a former justice of Ireland's Supreme Court, to hold a closed inquiry on the case. Carroll concluded that there was "clear and convincing evidence" Claxton had been assaulted.[34] But, Boutros-Ghali, citing "the best interests of the organization," embargoed the judge's report "and threatened Ms. Claxton with disciplinary action if she disobeyed the embargo."[35]

Eventually, lawyers for Claxton filed a lawsuit against Gomez, in part because Boutros-Ghali had "refused to make public the U.N.'s findings against Gomez or compensate her for damages," according to one report.[36] Claxton's lawyer, Ellen Yaroshevsky, said about Boutros-Ghali, "He's been biased from the beginning. When the allegation first surfaced he said, 'Mr. Gomez has our full support.' Then he tried to strong-arm her into dropping the case."[37]

Is the Claxton case unique? Another U.N. employee, a German woman named Gabriele Mussnig, was awarded more than two hundred thousand dollars in a sexual harassment case against the U.N.'s World Health Organization.[38] Moreover, *New York Daily News* reporters Gregory Beals and Rob Speyer reported that female employees of the U.N. in New York were reluctant to speak about sexual harassment there because they would face "immediate dismissal." They quoted one staffer, speaking anonymously, as saying, "You have to understand that there are people here with unlimited power. And, there is no real mechanism to control them." A female U.N. secretary said, "If you are not beautiful, they will change you for someone else. They are not interested in how you work, they are interested in how you look."[39]

Perhaps this helps explain why the U.N. suffers from chronic mismanagement.

Notes

1. The U.N. Report, *Washington Times* (21 January 1995): A9.

2. See Alan L. Keyes, "The United Nations," *Mandate for Leadership* (Washington, D.C.: The Heritage Foundation, 1989), 654.

3. Madeleine Albright, Hearing of the International Security, International Organizations and Human Rights Subcommittee of the House Foreign Affairs Committee, 17 May 1994.

4. "Talk Poor By Day, Live Rich By Night," *Sunday Times*, 15 August 1993.

5. Ibid.

6. CBS "60 Minutes," 19 September 1993, transcript prepared by Burrelle's Information Services.

7. Ibid.

8. Andrew J. Cowin, "Setting Priorities at the United Nations," *The Heritage Foundation* (26 July 1993), 4, 5.

9. Ibid.

10. William Drozdiak, "Rich, Poor Meet at Summit, And Go Their Separate Ways," *Washington Post* (12 March 1995).

11. Julia Preston, "The U.N.: Pushing 50 and Set in Its Ways," *Washington Post* (3 January 1995): 10.

12. "Another U.N. Conference," *Washington Post* (7 March 1995): A16.

13. Preston, "The U.N.," 1.

14. Julia Preston, "German At U.N. Is Focus of U.S. Political Dispute," *Washington Post* (28 March 1995): A11.

15. Facsimile transmission to author from Joan Hills, deputy director, U.N. Information Center, Washington, D.C., 8 November 1994.

16. Erskine Childers and Brian Urquhart, *Renewing the United Nations System* (The Ford Foundation and the Dag Hammarskjold Foundation, 1994), 29.

17. "The United Nations," *The Cato Handbook for Congress* (The Cato Institute, Washington, D.C. 1995), 287.

18. Ibid., 287, 288.

19. "Contractor Faces Harm," the U.N. report, *Washington Times* (11 March 1995): A8.

20. Reuters, "U.N. Opens Probe Into Contracts for Peace-keeping Forces Worldwide," *Washington Times* (23 July 1994).

21. Catherine Toups, "U.N. 'Wasting and Losing Millions of Dollars,' Investigators Say," *Washington Times* (24 December 1994): 1.

22. "U.N. Procurement Study Report," United Nations, December 1994, 1.

23. Ibid., 1.

24. Ibid., 1.

25. Iain Christie, "U.N. Troops Had Sex With Kids," Reuters News Agency, *Washington Times* (26 February 1994).

26. Marlise Simons, "The Littlest Prostitutes," *New York Times Magazine* (16 January 1994): 34.

27. Ibid., 35.

28. See Lambda Report, August 1993, 7.

29. Simons, "The Littlest Prostitutes," 35.

30. Toups, "U.N. 'Wasting and Losing,' " 1.

31. Julia Preston, "U.N. Wrestles With Sexual Harassment in Its Ranks," *Washington Post* (8 September 1994): A29.

32. Ciceil L. Gross, "Catherine Claxton vs. The U.N.," *New York Times* (15 September 1994): A23.

33. Preston, "U.N. Wrestles with Sexual Harassment," A29.

34. Ibid.

35. Gross, "Catherine Claxton," A23.

36. Salvatore Arena and Corky Siemaszko, "Staffer Slams Ex-Diplo in 2M Sex Harass Suit," *Daily News* (19 May 1994): 3c.

37. Ibid.

38. "U.N. Worker Wins Sex Harassment Case," *Baltimore Sun* (5 August 1994): 4a.

39. Gregory Beals and Rob Speyer, "A Whole Old World of Abuses," *Daily News* (19 May 1994): 3c.

The U.N.

5

Holy War

As the United Nations and its supporters struggle to preserve and expand the world body, they face a formidable foe: the Vatican. While Pope John Paul II may continue to get involved in U.N. conferences and activities, it is painfully clear that he regards the world body as an enemy, not a friend. The struggle involving the U.N. has taken on a spiritual dimension.

When in March of 1995 he issued a new encyclical covering moral issues such as abortion, he referred to various nations of the world engaging in a "conspiracy against life." In stark terms, the pope said humanity was caught in "a dramatic clash between good and evil, death and life, the 'culture of death' and the 'culture of life.'" A Catholic Bishop explained that John Paul was referring to the church's experiences at the September 1994 U.N. International Conference on Population and Development (ICPD) held in Cairo, Egypt, otherwise known as the Cairo conference.[1]

The Vatican attained special U.N. status as a so-called nongovernmental organization and a Permanent Observer state in 1964. As such, it cannot vote in U.N. General Assemblies but can participate fully in U.N. conferences. It did so in a history-making way in the Cairo event. For committed Catholics, the controversy demonstrated that the United Nations has taken sides against a spiritual leader who believes ultimate victory is guaranteed by his authority as God's personal representative on earth.

The role of Pope John Paul II in thwarting the draft agenda of that conference was recognized even by secular authorities such as *Time* magazine, which named him Man of the Year and declared, "He stands solidly against much that the secular world deems progressive: the notion, for example, that humans share with God the right to determine who will and will not be born."

In fact, of course, many of those in that "secular world" do not even believe in God. In the case of the U.N. Cairo conference, the pope confronted awesome secular powers in the so-called international birth control movement, the feminist movement, Russia, China, Cuba, and the Clinton administration—forces which do not share that power of life and death with God but reserve it unto themselves.

In his explosive book, *The Keys of This Blood*, Vatican insider Malachi Martin provides some important insights into the thinking of the pope, describing the Catholic leader as challenging "globalist organizations" which, in China and India, promote forced abortions and sterilization, as well as the United States government, which alone spends "up to half a billion dollars every year from the public treasury on stiffly promoted birth control methods." Martin says the pope sees the "methods and programs" of these forces as moving toward "a human condition that will be irreconcilable with Christian principles and irreconcilable, too, with the generally admitted principles of human dignity and rights."[2]

Martin says the pope attacks abortion, as well as sex education, hedonism, and godlessness, because he views them as part of a "new world culture" that is emerging under U.N. sponsorship. "He is carrying the battle into our State Department and into the United Nations because not only is he a religious leader, but he is a sovereign in his own right and has representatives in about 115 countries," Martin says.[3]

The battle goes back a long way. In the first papal address to the U.N. in 1965, Pope John Paul VI denounced efforts by governments to control and limit populations artificially.

> Your task is so to improve food production that there will be enough for all the tables of mankind, and not press for an artificial control of births, which would be irrational, so as to cut down the number of guests at the banquet of life.[4]

Pope John Paul II, in his book, *Crossing the Threshold of Hope*, condemned government-organized population control efforts as well. However, in acknowledging that "irresponsible global population growth" was also not acceptable, he added:

> The rate of population growth needs to be taken into consideration. The right path is that which the Church calls responsible parenthood; that is taught by the Church's family counseling programs. Responsible parenthood is the necessary condition for human love, and it is also the necessary condition for authentic conjugal love, because love cannot be irresponsible.[5]

The Catholic church holds that sexual intercourse has two purposes—"the good of the spouses themselves and the transmission of life." It also recognizes "methods of birth regulation based on self-observation and the use of infertile periods" but describes modern-day birth control methods as "intrinsically evil" because they attempt to "render procreation impossible."[6] The church also believes that:

> The state has a responsibility for its citizens' well-being. In this capacity it is legitimate for it to intervene to orient the demography of the population. This can be done by means of objective and respectful information, but certainly not by authoritarian, coercive measures.[7]

However, as the pope knows, authoritarian and coercive measures have indeed been implemented, with the support of the U.N. The sponsor of the Cairo event, the U.N. Population Fund (UNFPA for short—it originally included the word *activities*), has been operating since 1969 and specializes in funding state-sponsored birth control programs, including the provision of condoms, pills, and IUDs, in 136 countries. It is a subsidiary organ of the U.N. General Assembly and its 1992 budget was estimated at $231.6 million. In 1993, of the U.N.'s top ten commercial purchases, number nine was contraceptives at $30 million.

Its most controversial activity has been involvement in Communist China's policy of one child per family, which was implemented in the late 1970s. Prof. Julian L. Simon describes how it works.

> Its "family planning" one-child policy is pure coercion. It includes forcing IUD's into the wombs of 100 million women against their will; mandatory X-rays every three months to ensure that the IUD's have not been removed, causing who knows what genetic damage; coercion to abort if women get pregnant anyway, and economic punishment if couples evade the abortionist.[8]

An official of the Population Council explained, "China's view is that reproductive rights belong to the state; reproductive rights are not something for an individual or even a family to possess."[9] The "economic punishment" alluded to by Simon was described by CNN reporter Mike Chinoy.

> In the cities, family planning is enforced through a controversial system of rewards and punishments. If you violate the one-child policy, you could jeopardize your job, your housing, your medical benefits, and your food subsidies.[10]

Moreover, custom in China demands that couples produce male heirs. The result, according to the *New York Times*:

> The preference for boys has meant that millions of Chinese girls have not survived to adulthood because of poor nutrition, inadequate medical care, desertion and even murder at the hands of their parents.[11]

One of the technologies used to produce a male heir in China as well as India is sex selection abortion. Female fetuses are simply identified and aborted. In China alone, according to an article in the journal *Science*, male live births have exceeded those of females by amounts far greater than those which occur naturally. The article said the imbalance is about 1 million males per year after 2010.

> Infant and unborn females thus appear to have a disparately low value in countries that constitute 40% of the world's population. The status of these females deserves scholarly attention, ethical and moral concern, and governmental initiatives. In the longer term, masculinization of births will result in large cohorts of young unmarried males, posing social and cultural challenges in countries that are already undergoing rapid economic and political change. The trends we note are likely to complicate efforts

to increase the social and economic status of women and their control over reproductive decisions.[12]

The extent of the UNFPA's involvement in the China policy was described by Rep. Chris Smith.

> Since 1979 to today, the UNFPA has vigorously defended China's barbaric population control program despite the fact that the PRC relies heavily on forced abortion and forced sterilization to achieve its results. The UNFPA has poured over $150 million into China's program, its personnel work side-by-side with Beijing's cadres and on numerous occasions in a myriad of fora the UNFPA has whitewashed massive violations of human rights in that repressed country.[13]

Effective 1 June 1995, the Chinese government went one step further, implementing a law forcing couples with hereditary diseases to be sterilized before marriage. Such a policy is a clear example of eugenics—attempting to improve the human condition through genetic or scientific manipulation.

Steven Mosher, author of *One Woman's Fight Against China's One Child Policy* (HarperCollins, 1994), says the Chinese program, which promises to get worse in the years ahead, has resulted in "women's reproductive rights being violated on a massive scale."[14]

Nevertheless, the U.N. scheduled its Fourth World Conference on Women in Beijing during September 1995. The U.N. defied the Vatican and granted the pro-abortion group Catholics for a Free Choice permission to participate in the conference. The Vatican argued that it was wrong for the group to identify itself as Catholic since it opposed Catholic teachings. But, the agenda of the group goes further than abortion. Catholics for a Free Choice has even received funding from the Playboy Foundation, an arm of the company that publishes *Playboy* magazine.

The U.N.'s complicity in the Chinese program helps demonstrate the world body's penchant for totalitarianism. But, it also suggests that if world government comes, it could easily come through population control programs.

However, it wasn't until Pres. Clinton nominated Dr. Henry W. Foster, Jr., as surgeon general of the United States that many people realized how far the United States had already come down this same road. The record showed that he had performed an unknown number of surgical abortions (as many as seven hundred), had supervised a study that used drugs to induce abortions, and had endorsed fetal experimentation and human embryo research. He had also engaged in the involuntary sterilization of the retarded, at a time when federal regulations banned the use of federal funds for such procedures.[15]

In addition, the Family Research Council charged that it appeared that Foster had knowledge of what is perhaps the most infamous medical experiment in American history, the Tuskegee Syphilis Study, and did nothing to speak up for the rights of those who were subjected to it.[16] This hideous experiment involved deliberately withholding treatment for hundreds of syphilitic black men—without their knowledge or consent—for forty years. The purpose of the experiment, conducted in part by the U.S. government, was to examine the effects after death of untreated syphilis.

Focusing on just a few of the shocking items in Foster's background, Judie Brown, president of American Life League, asked:

> Isn't it possible that Dr. Foster has a philosophy based on eugenics, which would explain

why he would sterilize mentally incompetent women and abort children who were deemed to be less than perfect human beings?[17]

Journalist Suzanne Rini, author of *Beyond Abortion*, believes the United States has laid the groundwork for a eugenics program through such procedures as fetal experimentation (the removal of organs and body tissue from human infants scheduled for abortion), human embryo research and in vitro fertilization. She says other practices such as cloning of human beings, hybridizing humans with other species, making embryos solely for research and human organ "farming" are on the way.[18]

The answer to the question of whether Foster personally embraced a philosophy of eugenics could lie in the nature of his association with the Planned Parenthood Federation of America (PPFA), a government-funded chain of birth control clinics that performed 130,277 abortions in 1992.[19] Foster served on national PPFA's board, as well as the board of a local PPFA affiliate that went to court to overturn a law requiring parental consent when teenagers under eighteen years old seek abortion.[20]

To many Americans, the name Planned Parenthood implies responsibility, even family values. However, it was founded back in 1915 by Margaret Sanger under the name of the American Birth Control League. The name was changed for public relations reasons to Planned Parenthood Federation of America in 1942 and an international arm was formed as well. Elasha Drogin, whose biography of Sanger calls her the *Father of Modern Society*, describes her influence.

> The influence of Margaret Sanger's International Planned Parenthood Federation on the contemporary world is so great that one can say that its slogans and values have become

exactly those of modern Western civilization and are rapidly becoming the morals which dominate the rest of the world. In 1900 the world society would in no way have held the values of Margaret Sanger and Planned Parenthood to be anything other than a form of contemptible utopianism. If a citizen of 1900 were told by a time machine traveler that in just 75 years birth control devices and chemicals would be a socially highly approved normal manner of life along with worldwide approval of abortion as a back up for contraceptive failure, our 1900 citizen would be shocked into unconsciousness. If, upon revival, we were to tell him that by 1978 most forms of promiscuity and pornography had become generally acceptable by nearly everybody as a result of the effectiveness of mechanical and chemical contraception whose complications are taken care of by abortions, surgical sterilization, and hysterectomies, one wonders if our 1900 citizen could have survived the surprise.[21]

Sanger, who died in 1966, was a revolutionary Socialist and anti-Christian activist who received massive foundation grants to support her work. Personally, she was sexually promiscuous and dabbled in the occult.[22] A sympathetic biography said she became "rabidly anti-Catholic as she grew older."[23]

A central focus of her activities was getting the U.S. federal government to endorse and promote her work, with George Grant reporting that Sanger testified before several congressional committees, "advocating the liberalization of contraceptive prescription laws" and fighting for "the incorporation of reproductive control into state programs as a form of social planning."[24]

Biographer Ellen Chesler admits that Sanger, "[w]ithout any apparent concern for the potential of abuse," supported state initiatives in the 1920s and 1930s to forcibly sterilize individuals believed to be carrying inherited deficiencies, such as mental retardation or insanity. One such law, authorizing the involuntary sterilization of inmates in state institutions in Virginia, was actually upheld by the U.S. Supreme Court in 1927.[25]

The clear intention of the birth control effort from the beginning was not to give individuals the right to make decisions, in the privacy of their own bedrooms, but rather to "empower" government to regulate and control the human species for its own purposes. This is a philosophy that works to the benefit of totalitarian regimes, be they Communist, Nazi, or Fascist.

With the power of government to back them, some of the early slogans of the birth control movement are positively frightening today: "More children from the fit, less from the unfit—that is the chief aim of birth control," and "Birth Control: to create a race of thoroughbreds." Sanger's own book, *The Pivot of Civilization*, included references to eliminating "human weeds" and sterilizing "genetically inferior races."[26]

However, the U.S. government would not be the first to implement her policies on a massive and brutal scale. That task was left to Adolf Hitler's Third Reich. Grant notes that Sanger

> had become closely associated with the scientists and theorists who put together Nazi Germany's "race purification" program. She had openly endorsed the euthanasia, sterilization, abortion, and infanticide programs of the early Reich. She published a number of articles in *The Birth Control Review* that mirrored Hitler's Aryan-White Supremacist rhetoric. She even commissioned Dr. Ernst Rudin, the director of the Nazi Medical Experimentation Program, to write for *The Review* himself.[27]

But, Sanger backpedaled from her support of the Nazi programs once the grisly details came to light.

The major breakthroughs for the birth control movement in the United States came in the 1960s and 1970s as Sanger was nearing the end of her life. One year before her death, in 1965, the U.S. Supreme Court in *Griswold v. Connecticut* overturned a law forbidding contraception and created a so-called constitutional right to privacy. This case was supported by the American Civil Liberties Union and Planned Parenthood.[28]

In 1972, the court expanded on this ruling in *Baird v. Eisenstadt* and, one year later, utilized the so-called right to privacy to legalize abortion on demand in the *Roe v. Wade* decision. These cases were financially assisted by the Playboy Foundation, an arm of the company that publishes *Playboy* magazine.[29] Playboy has also been a significant funder of Planned Parenthood.[30] The involvement of *Playboy* in funding such causes certainly raises questions about the motivations of all concerned—whether, in fact, abortion and "family planning" are really designed to encourage sexual promiscuity and eliminate personal responsibility. In fact, some feminists say that *Playboy* supports abortion rights to keep women sexually attractive and available to men.

From a professed desire simply to make birth control devices available to people in the privacy of their own homes, the movement has evolved into a campaign with government backing financed by taxpayers that attempts to force "family planning" on everyone through clinics in communities and even public schools.

Since 1970, through the Family Planning Services and Population Research Act, Title X appropriations of the Public Health Service Act, Planned Parenthood itself has received tens of millions of dollars from the

American taxpayer. By 1992, a year in which more than 1.9 million women received contraceptive services at Planned Parenthood clinics, it topped $200 million.

Moreover, it didn't seem to matter which administration, Democratic or Republican, was in power. "During the twelve years of pro-life Republican Administrations [1980–92], funding for Planned Parenthood's lascivious Title X programs actually tripled," Grant says.[31] An analysis of funding for Planned Parenthood over an eighteen month period, 1993-1994, showed "government grants" rising to $238.2 million, 34 percent of the organization's total revenue.[32]

But, Grant argues that Planned Parenthood's ultimate take from the federal treasury through agencies such as the Agency for International Development (AID), as well as the U.N. Population Fund and other groups, amounts to "billions."[33]

The first big exception to the bipartisan policy in support of Planned Parenthood came in 1984 when prolife President Ronald Reagan's so-called Mexico City Policy prevailed at a U.N. population conference in Mexico City. The policy held that there should be no government funding for programs promoting abortion as birth control. Planned Parenthood was outraged.

The Clinton administration was determined to change that. As one of his first official acts, Clinton said that his administration would provide political and economic support to the UNFPA and IPPF and would use the Cairo conference as an opportunity to overturn the 1984 Mexico City Policy.

Bracing for that conference, Clinton Undersecretary of State for Global Affairs Timothy E. Wirth claimed that, "All but 17 of the 189 U.N. countries permit abortions," implying that those opposed to abortion were a small fringe group. Douglas Johnson, legislative director of the National Right to Life Committee, countered that ninety-five nations covering 37 percent of the world's population had laws protecting the unborn in most circumstances.

In Cairo, where 180 countries were represented, the U.N. was preparing to go further than it had ever gone before. Not only did it endorse the "provision of universal access to family planning and reproductive services," a euphemism for abortion, it stated there were "various concepts" of family, all of them equally valid. Critics saw this as an implicit endorsement of homosexual marriages and sexual promiscuity.

Not surprisingly, J. Michael Waller, who covered the conference for the *American Spectator*, reported that the event was dominated by Planned Parenthood:

> Three years of preparation for the Cairo conference were clothed in a veneer of openness and pluralism, but in reality were tightly controlled by a small group dominated by the United Nations Population Fund, the International Planned Parenthood Federation, [IPPF] and allied Americans activists. . . .
>
> The case of ICPD leaders reveals a revolving door of population control careerists and the contraceptive and supranational financial industries that stand to benefit from their activism. . . .
>
> ICPD Secretary General Nafis Sadik is executive director of the UNFPA and is formerly with IPPF. Undersecretary General Joseph Chamie is director of the U.N. Population Division. . . . The chairman of the committee that wrote the draft Programme of Action at the prepatory conferences and controlled the amendment process for the final document at Cairo was Fred Sai, a former World Bank

population adviser who is presently IPPF President. . . .

Planned Parenthood had a massive fifth-column presence [at the conference]. According to internal IPPF documents obtained in Cairo, the organization or its national affiliates had their own individuals on the official government delegations of no fewer than 26 and as many as 58 countries; the precise number could not be determined because ICPD officials failed to provide journalists with a complete listing of delegates. Some of these countries were too poor to send their own envoys, so Planned Parenthood and U.N. agencies paid for their chosen delegates to represent them, putting the individuals up in some of Cairo's most expensive hotels. At least 33 IPPF directors and staffers also attended, bringing Planned Parenthood's Cairo contingent to more than 200 trained organizers and lobbyists, all with a huge financial stake in the outcome. The main enemy—the Holy See, as the Vatican is known in diplomacy—had only 17 delegates.

So incestuous were the relationships that it was hard to tell whose conference it really was. Initiated by the U.N., the ICPD was dominated by the Clinton Administration, whose point man was Undersecretary of State for Global Affairs Timothy E. Wirth, a former Senator who had been a local Planned Parenthood board member in his native Colorado.[34]

The pope was extremely alarmed at what was being planned. In March of 1994, he met with Nafis Sadik and, face to face, criticized her and the draft program endorsing abortion and redefining the family. In public appearances, the pope was outspoken, saying that the U.N. conference was designed to "destroy the family" and was the "snare of the devil." He told parishioners at a church in Rome:

> I am going back to the Vatican to combat a project prepared by the United Nations, which want to destroy the family. I say simply no, no. Think again. Convert your hearts. If you are the United Nations, you must not destroy.[35]

If the U.N. endorsed abortion as an international "right," Alfonso Cardinal Lopez Trujillo, head of the Pontifical Council for the Family, said the Cairo conference could lead to "the most disastrous massacre in history."[36]

In June, the pope met with President Clinton. Afterward, Vatican spokesman Joaquin Navarro-Valls said the most important part of the meeting involved the upcoming Cairo conference. He said, "In this regard, the pope made an appeal to the responsibility of a great nation such as America, whose origin and historical development have always promoted ethical values that are basic to every culture."[37]

Of course, the pope knew full well that the great nation of America had changed radically since the U.S. Supreme Court had legalized abortion. He also knew that the Clinton administration had come into office in 1992 with the support of both the abortion rights and gay rights movements, and that some of Clinton's very first actions in office were designed to protect and expand those "rights." By the time of this meeting, the pope was also aware that Clinton's Surgeon General Joycelyn Elders' pro-homosexual, pro-abortion and pro-drug statements had enraged many Americans, including U.S. Catholic leaders who had implicitly urged her firing.

In retrospect, the pope's discussion with Clinton amounted to a warning. John Paul, who became pope

in 1978, had worked closely with the Reagan administration on several different issues. Opposition to
communism was one. Another was opposition to the
population control movement that Clinton was to
embrace. Indeed, the Vatican and the Reagan administration had, in effect, become partners in making
sure the Mexico City Policy was adopted at the 1984
U.N. population conference in Mexico City. As such,
it was to be expected that the Vatican would vigor-
ously oppose any Clinton administration plan to endorse making abortion a government-guaranteed
"right" at the 1994 Cairo event.

President Clinton, however, claimed to be mysti-
fied that his efforts were encountering such strenuous
opposition. At one point, Clinton reportedly said to
Rep. Chris Smith, "I don't like how we're positioned
with the Vatican."[38] Following that, Vice President Al
Gore, the leader of the U.S. delegation to the conference, changed his stance, declaring that, "The United
States has not sought, does not seek and will not seek
an international right to abortion."[39]

Looking back on the controversy, Dr. James Dobson, the president of Focus on the Family, would say:

> Thanks largely to the efforts of Pope John Paul
> II and *very few* evangelicals [emphasis in origi-
> nal], the conference ended in controversy and
> disunity. It could have been a disaster for the
> family around the world if the planners had
> their way. Those same policies that were being
> promoted in Cairo have severely damaged our
> own culture.[40]

Rep. Christopher H. Smith, an official observer at
the Cairo conference, had similar sentiments:

> The final conference document, called
> Programme of Action, was, all things consid-
> ered, a remarkable victory for global pro-life

forces and the 100 countries throughout the world that protect the lives of their unborn children.

Led by a highly skilled and tenacious Vatican delegation, dozens of African, Central and South American countries joined Muslim states to resist abortion lobby bullying, despite vigorous opposition from the Clinton delegation at prepatory meetings in New York and Cairo.

The final conference document affirmed all nations' "sovereignty" to protect and cherish the precious lives of unborn babies, and said that "in no case should abortion be promoted as a method of family planning."[41]

Time magazine, which named the pope its Man of the Year for 1994 for opposing the U.N., described the pope's efforts:

For nine days the Vatican delegates, under his direction, lobbied and filibustered; they kept their Latin American bloc in line and struck up alliances with Islamic nations opposed to abortion. In the end, the Pope won.[42]

Some observers believe that the Vatican got involved in the conflict simply because of the issue of abortion. There is no question that the Roman Catholic church regards abortion as a moral evil. Pope John Paul II has referred to it as such.[43] He has also stated that abortion is a violation of God's commandment against killing.[44]

In remarks delivered before President and Mrs. Clinton and Vice President and Mrs. Gore, who are "prochoice" on abortion, Mother Teresa of Calcutta said:

If we accept that a mother can kill even her own child, how can we tell other people not to

kill each other? . . . Any country that accepts
abortion is not teaching its people to love, but
to use any violence to get what they want.[45]

Mother Teresa's description of abortion as violence was a reference to how abortions are performed–
either through razorblade-tipped suction devices or
injections of chemical poisons.

In one sense, the Vatican's campaign can be explained by the recognition that the U.N. had betrayed
its own statements in favor of the rights of the unborn. For example, the U.N. Convention on the Rights
of the Child, though objectionable in many respects,
nevertheless included in its preamble a recognition
that

> everyone is entitled to all the rights and free-
> doms set forth therein, without distinction of
> any kind, such as race, colour, sex, language,
> religion, political or other opinion, national or
> social origin, property, *birth or other status.* (em-
> phasis added)[46]

But, the pope's concern went far beyond the issue
of U.N. hypocrisy and abortion. The Vatican was blunt
about the stakes involved, saying, "The Holy See is
well aware that the future of humanity is under discussion."[47] Some saw apocalyptic overtones in the pope's
comments that the devil himself was trying to manipulate the U.N.'s Cairo conference.

Regarding the pope's general vision of world
events, *Newsweek* has written, "The Pope is driven by
his foreboding that the world is heading toward a
moral apocalypse." Indeed, there are signs indicating
that the pope believes that humanity is entering a
crisis stage in which divine intervention may occur. It
is significant that, in the past, Vatican representative
Cardinal L. Ciappis has praised the book, *The Antichrist,* by Father Vincent Miceli, which labels abortion

as the work of the forerunners of the Antichrist, the personal representative of Satan.[48]

Some evangelical Christians see the issue in the same way. In fact, some believe abortion is more than just the planned destruction of a human life, but a form of child sacrifice with Satanic overtones. They point to the "blasphemous" comments of an ordained episcopal priest, active in the feminist movement, who said, "If women were in charge, abortion would be a sacrament—an occasion of deep and serious and sacred meaning."[49]

It is significant that, at the Cairo conference, Russia and President Clinton's America stood shoulder to shoulder. "Russia is categorically against a ban on abortion," declared a Russian representative at the Cairo conference.[50] Whether it's the old Soviet Union or modern-day Russia, they have one thing in common with the U.S. today—abortion on demand. In fact, Russia today has the highest abortion rate in the world. In 1992, it was 3.3 million, or two abortions for each live birth.[51]

Despite their perceived differences today, Russia and Communist Cuba share this policy. At a 1994 conference of Latin American leaders, fifteen out of the sixteen countries attending reaffirmed their anti-abortion policies. The only dissenter was Communist Cuba's Fidel Castro.[52] In fact, according to one report from the Communist-controlled island: "Cuba is using more than sunshine and beaches to lure foreign tourists here. Foreigners are offered: plastic surgery—heart, kidney or bone marrow transplants—even abortions."[53]

Yet, there is reason to believe that Cuba will soon be joined in its proabortion advocacy by another country in Latin America and the Caribbean—Haiti.

As reported by journalist William Norman Grigg, who covered the Cairo conference, a man who identified himself as a representative of the United Na-

tions Association posed the following question to Vice
President Gore during a question-and-answer session
at the Cairo conference.

> Why can't the United States send huge hospi-
> tal ships to Haiti to deliver good medicine to
> an impoverished people? Giving good medi-
> cine establishes confidence in the doctors, which
> could then get an agreement to have small
> families, to accept contraceptives, sterilization,
> and abortion.[54]

Gore's answer, after first evading the question and
then consulting with U.S. AID Chief Brian Atwood,
was that the U.N. and the "international community"
would make an effort to address "a broad range of
problems in Haiti." Grigg commented, "It is significant that Gore did not reject outright the suggestion
that U.N. 'aid' to Haiti may be used as leverage to
compel Haitians to accept sterilization, abortion and
other 'family planning' options—perhaps because such
linkage is a common population control practice."[55]

The Vatican has to be aware that such linkage is
possible, even probable, because the Clinton administration and the U.N. restored Fr. Jean-Bertrand Aristide
to power in Haiti. This was another direct affront to
the Vatican.

Still officially a Roman Catholic priest, Aristide
was dismissed from the Church's Salesian Order in
1988 for "incitement to hatred and violence ... and
profanation of the liturgy."[56] Aristide became known
as an advocate of "liberation theology," a mixture of
Christianity and Marxism that Malachi Martin calls a
"perfectly faithful exercise" of the principles of Italian
Communist Antonio Gramsci, who emphasized cultural penetration of Western institutions.

After Aristide was elected president of Haiti in
December 1990, a pro-Aristide mob burned down a

church and threatened the life of Haitian Catholic Archbishop Francois Ligonde. But, it was Aristide's violations of the Haitian Constitution that caused the Haitian military to overthrow him in September 1991. Significantly, the Vatican was the only state in the world to recognize the new anti-Aristide regime. That's because the pope understands what Aristide represents and who supports him.

Notes

1. Laurie Goodstein, "Nations Conspire 'Against Life,' Pope Says," *Washington Post* (31 March 1995): 1.

2. Malachi Martin, *The Keys of This Blood* (New York: Simon and Schuster, 1990), 340.

3. Radio interview with author, "Point of View Radio Talk Show with Marlin Maddoux," 1 August 1994.

4. Denise Shannon, "All Roads Lead to Cairo," *Conscience*, (Winter 1994–95), 14–15.

5. John Paul II, *Crossing the Threshold of Hope* (New York: Alfred A. Knopf, 1994), 208.

6. *Catechism of the Catholic Church* (U.S. Catholic Conference, 1994), 570.

7. Ibid.

8. Julian L. Simon, "The Population Distraction," *New York Times* (21 August 1994).

9. As quoted in Mike Chinoy's "The People Bomb," Cable News Network, 28 May 1992.

10. Ibid.

11. Philip Shenon, *New York Times* (16 August 1994): A8.

12. Shripad Tuljapurkar, Nan Li, Marcus W. Feldman, "High Sex Ratios in China's Future," *Science* (10 February 1995): 874–876.

13. Rep. Chris Smith, "A Call to Leaders in Developing Countries to Resist Clinton's Pressure to Abandon Unborn Babies," 8 April 1994.

14. Steven W. Mosher, "China's Grim One-Child Rule Get(s) Worse," *Washington Times* (4 April 1995): 19.

15. Charles Krauthammer, "A Troubling Medical Act," *Washington Post* (17 February 1995): A25.

16. "Tuskegee Study and Henry Foster," Family Research Council, undated.

17. Judie Brown, "Fact Sheet: Henry Foster, Jr., M.D.," 2.

18. See "Creating a Master Race," Interview with Suzanne Rini, *The Free American* (Freedom Alliance), October 1994.

19. Joyce Price, "Focus on Foster Endangers Planned Parenthood Funds," *Washington Times* (6 March 1995): A3.

20. Deborah Orin, "Abortion Foes Hope Parental-Consent Flap Will Sink Foster," *New York Post* (15 February 1995).

21. Elasha Drogin, *Margaret Sanger: Father of Modern Society* (Coarsegold, California: CUL Publications, 1979), 22.

22. George Grant, *Grand Illusions: The Legacy of Planned Parenthood* (Franklin, Tennessee: Adroit Press, 1988), 55, 61.

23. Ellen Chesler, *Woman of Valor: Margaret Sanger and the Birth Control Movement in America* (New York: Simon & Schuster, 1992), 15.

24. Grant, *Grand Illusions*, 61.

25. Chesler, *Woman of Valor*, 215, 216.

26. Grant, *Grand Illusions*, 59.

27. Grant, *Grand Illusions*, 61.

28. Robert H. Bork, *The Tempting of America* (New York: Simon & Schuster, 1990), 96.

29. Cliff Kincaid, *The Playboy Foundation: A Mirror of the Culture?* (Washington, D.C.: Capital Research Center, 1992), 22, 23.

30. Ibid.

31. Grant, *Grand Illusions*, 29.

32. Price, "Focus on Foster Endangers," A3.

33. Grant, *Grand Illusions*, 29.

34. J. Michael Waller, "What Really Happened in Cairo," written for *The American Spectator* undated., 7.

35. Shannon, *Conscience*, 5.

36. As quoted by Alan Cowell, "Vatican Attacks Population Stand Supported by U.S.," *New York Times* (9 August 1994).

37. John Thavis, quoted in "Pope Urges U.S. To Defend Human Life," Catholic News Service, *The Catholic Standard* (9 June 1994): 2.

38. Waller, "What Really Happened," 7.

39. Ibid.

40. Dr. James Dobson, "Dear Friends" letter, January 1995, Colorado Springs, Colorado.

41. Rep. Christopher Smith, "U.N. Abortion Agenda Stopped," *Christian American* (October 1994): 10.

42. "Man of the Year," *Time* (26 December 1994–2 January 1995): 56.

43. John Paul II, *Crossing the Threshold*, 205.

44. Ibid.

45. As quoted by Cal Thomas, "Truth, Power and Abortion," *Miami Herald* (10 February 1994).

46. "Convention on the Rights of the Child," United Nations, (5 December 1989): 3.

47. Cowell, "Vatican Attacks."

48. Available from Roman Catholic Books, P.O. Box 2286, Ft. Collins, Colorado, 80522-2286.

49. See "Massacre of Innocence," Reel to Real Ministries, P.O. Box 44290, Pittsburgh, Pennsylvania, 15205.

50. Quoted in "Abortion a Way of Life Russian Women Admit," by Olivia Ward, *Toronto Star* (15 September 1994): A19.

51. "Russia's Spiritual Wilderness," *Policy Review*, The Heritage Foundation, (Fall 1994): 12.

52. Brian Robertson, *Washington Times* (16 August 1994): 8A.

53. Juan J. Walte, "Cuba Lures Tourists with Sun, Sand and Surgery," *USA Today* (19 August 1991): 5A.

54. William Norman Grigg, "A Covenant With Death," *The New American* (17 October 1994): 11.

55. Ibid.

56. Lawrence T. DiRita, "Aristide in His Own words," The Heritage Foundation (16 September 1994).

The U.N.

6

Comrades

Considering that the United Nations is supposed to be open to all "peace-loving nations," a matter of critical concern is how the Soviet Union came to belong to it and why the United States has not left the world body in protest over communism's legacy of killing more than one hundred million people. The short answer is that we have been—and continue to be—fooled.

To put it charitably, President Clinton is the worst fool of all. His May 9 trip to Moscow, rather than London, to celebrate V-E Day was a national disgrace. Clinton celebrated the fiftieth anniversary of the allied victory over Hitler's Germany by clinking glasses with Russian President Boris Yeltsin, a man who, when he was sober, looked the other way as Russian troops conducted a Nazi-like military campaign against civilians in the Chechnyan region of the former Soviet Union. More than twenty-five thousand civilians had been killed at the time of Clinton's trip.

Yeltsin, the record shows, approved continuing Russian intelligence operations against the United States in the person of Aldrich Ames, acquiesced while the Russian military continues production of biological and chemical weapons, and approved the sale of a nuclear reactor to Iran to enable the Islamic state to construct a nuclear weapon.

Yeltsin also refuses to get to the bottom of reports that American POWs remain in the former Soviet Union. As many as ten American POWs in Vietnam— one of them, perhaps, who went in place of Bill Clinton—were transferred to the Soviet gulag, according to Malcolm McConnell's book, *Inside Hanoi's Secret Archives*. McConnell says these POWs had strategic and technical knowledge useful to the Soviets. This transfer was consistent, McConnell says, with Soviet policy during the Korean War, when over two hundred American POWS were sent to the Soviet Union.

According to defense analyst and author Joseph Douglass, Jr., the story is more hideous than that. In articles appearing in *Conservative Review*, based on information provided by a former high-level Czech official, Gen. Maj. Jan Sejna, Douglass described a top secret Soviet intelligence operation that began in the Korean War and continued through the Vietnam War that tested chemical and biological agents and mind-control drugs on American POWs. Some of these tests were conducted on POWs shipped to the Soviet Union, he says.

Despite all of this, the Clinton administration had budgeted more than $100 million for housing for Russian Army officers, supposedly as an inducement for them to return to Moscow, when our own troops and their families increasingly have to go on food stamps to survive.

Of course, Clinton's trip to Moscow was only designed to celebrate the allied victory over Hitler. In fact, however, as Clinton was supposed to learn at Oxford, the Soviet Union got into the war only after Hitler turned on Stalin. History shows both had signed a nonaggression pact—a deal that provoked the war itself. At the time of the signing of the Hitler-Stalin pact, Soviet foreign Minister Molotov said, "fascism is a matter of taste." Indeed, Hitler and Stalin came to blows not because they were different but because they were similar. Both were totalitarian and both had dreams of world domination.

Trying to defend the Clinton Moscow trip, the hapless White House chief of staff, Leon Panetta, said that Clinton's intention was to recognize the Russian contribution to the war effort, that twenty million Russians were killed during the war—"more," Panetta continued, "than all of the Allies combined." But, as columnist Ralph De Toledano pointed out, several million of these were slaughtered by the Soviets themselves. Moreover, many of the Soviets died because Stalin refused certain kinds of American aid—such as American planes refueling at Soviet airfields to carry out bombing raids on Nazi supply lines—that would have alerted the Soviet people themselves to the fact that the Americans were an integral part of the war effort. By using the "twenty million" figure, Panetta was repeating the big lie of Stalin himself, who wanted the Soviet people to think the Americans were doing virtually nothing to stop Hitler.

After the Soviets got into the war, moreover, they continued their espionage operations against us, demonstrating that they still regarded the U.S. as the main enemy.

> Despite the Soviet need for American and British participation in the war, Soviet intelligence still operated against the Allies. Through such intelligence efforts the secrets of the atom bomb were obtained for the Soviet Union. The postwar Soviet military threat against Western Europe based on Soviet atomic weapons was the result of their successful espionage.[1]

After the war, the United Nations came into being. The name "United Nations" was coined by President Franklin D. Roosevelt and first used in the Declaration of United Nations of January 1, 1942 by those countries, including the Soviet Union, fighting the Axis Powers during World War II. Ex-KGB agent Anatoliy Golitsyn, whose 1984 book *New Lies for Old* forecast the crumbling of the Berlin Wall, said the signing of this pact by the Soviet Union was a strategic "deception" that was designed to be "seen as part of the effort to raise Western expectations of favorable developments in the Soviet Union."[2]

But, the Roosevelt administration, penetrated by Soviet agents, was predisposed that way. The Soviet agents included Harry Hopkins, a key adviser to President Roosevelt, and high-ranking State Department official Alger Hiss, who was identified as a member of a secret Communist cell by defector Whittaker Chambers. Hiss was later convicted of perjury for denying he was a Soviet spy. (He was charged with perjury because the statute of limitations had expired on his purported espionage activities.)

Conferences in Teheran and Yalta dealing with post-war issues included Hopkins and Hiss as American advisers and produced "Soviet triumphs" that resulted in the Soviets recovering their ill-gotten gains of the Nazi-Soviet pact, extending their influence over Eastern Europe, obtaining billions of dollars in Western aid, and laying the foundation for the creation of the United Nations organization.[3]

The Soviets had big plans for Hiss. In his book, *KGB: The Inside Story*, Oleg Gordievsky, the Soviet KGB's former station chief in London, explained:

> Hiss's career appeared to offer the NKVD [the predecessor of the KGB] a remarkable opportunity within the new United Nations. In April

1945 he became temporary secretary-general of the UN "organizing conference" at San Francisco. Unsurprisingly, [the then-Soviet Ambassador in Washington Andrei] Gromyko expressed "a very high regard for Alger Hiss, particularly for his fairness and impartiality." He told [U.S. Secretary of State] Stettenius that he would be happy for Hiss to become temporary secretary-general of the UN constituent assembly, a position that might well have led to his appointment as first permanent secretary-general of the United Nations.[4]

The U.N. organizing conference, held from 25 April to 26 June, produced a U.N. charter but the organization itself didn't officially come into existence until 24 October, when the document was ratified by nationalist China, France, the Soviet Union, the United Kingdom, the United States, and a majority of other signatories.

Just five years later, Stalin demonstrated his peace-loving commitment when he conspired with the North Korean Communists to launch an invasion of South Korea. A former North Korean ambassador to the Soviet Union, Li San-Cho, confirmed that Stalin consulted with North Korean dictator Kim Il-Sung before the 1950 invasion and decided to concoct a South Korean military incursion as an excuse for the Communist assault.[5]

A South Korean scholar who examined recently disclosed Soviet documents from that period say they confirm that the invasion was launched after Stalin gave his approval. The scholar said that, with the victory of communism in China and Moscow's success (through espionage) in breaking the American nuclear monopoly, "Stalin concluded that the international climate had now turned favorable."[6]

Defenders of the U.N. contend that the organization took decisive action against the Communist invasion of the South. Former KGB agent Golitsyn agrees
that the "unexpectedly prompt and effective U.N. intervention" threw the Communists off-guard. But, he
says this was because Stalin did not consult fully with
Chinese Communist ruler Mao Tse Tung on the invasion and had to bring "severe Soviet pressure" on him
to send Chinese "volunteers" into the fighting.

For the West, the critical point came in 1951,
when U.N. forces were on the offensive and Gen.
Douglas MacArthur was calling for total victory, including air and ground attacks on the Chinese main-
land. MacArthur was then relieved of his command by
President Truman and cease-fire discussions began in
response to a proposal by the Soviet Union for U.N.-
sponsored truce talks. In the Korean conflict, wrote
retired Maj. Gen. John K. Singlaub, America "accepted
a strange new concept: limited war."[7]

The concept of "limited war" was also applied in
the Vietnam conflict, started by North Vietnamese
Communist Ho Chi Minh, albeit without U.N. involvement. Gen. Norman Schwartzkopf, commander of
Operation Desert Storm, has written that one of the
reasons the U.S. lost in Vietnam was a failure to ob-
tain "international legitimacy," such as the U.N., for
our intervention. Others contend the United States
lost the war because there was a failure of will and
because an objective of total victory was not pursued.

In any case, U.N. backing for the Vietnam War
was not practical because the U.N. was already undergoing a dramatic transformation from the time when
it was considered an organization dominated by the
United States. The change was dramatized when Soviet leader Nikita Khrushchev traveled to New York in
September 1960, yanked off his shoe, and pounded it

on his desk at the U.N. General Assembly. In a speech less than one month after this provocative appearance, Khrushchev issued a threat:

> We, the socialist countries, are today in a minority in the United Nations, but this situation might change. Today we are in a minority, but tomorrow, as we foretell you, we will be in the majority. Hence, you must not abuse a temporary majority in the United Nations to impose decisions on the minority because, I repeat, this is not a parliament.[8]

In effect, the Soviets and their Third World allies were openly advertising their takeover of the world body. This was "in-your-face" diplomacy. This is something that had been forecast by French President Charles De Gaulle, who warned President Eisenhower about making a "fetish" out of the world body.

Speaking at a 1985 conference on Soviet propaganda and disinformation, Paul Seabury of the University of California at Berkeley said that the West was losing the war of ideas with the Communists because we had been unable to effectively counter their "lies," which they were spreading through U.N. agencies. A summary of his remarks said:

> A case in point is the intellectual transformation that has occurred in the United Nations in the 40 years since its organization under American auspices. No longer is the U.N. considered a pawn of the United States. Now, with the growth of the UN's membership, the United States is routinely in the minority on fundamental issues, and often in a minority of two or three members. Seabury wondered what role the Soviet Union might have played in bringing about this transformation. His impression was that the Soviets have been very busy there

over the past few years. Certainly many of the
items of business raised in the UN correspond
to Soviet ideology.[9]

The U.N., in short, had become a major base for
Soviet propaganda and intelligence activities. John
Barron, author of the authoritative book, *KGB: The
Secret Work of Soviet Secret Agents*, noted that a top-
secret KGB textbook "stresses the value of the United
Nations as a clandestine base." The KGB textbook,
entitled *The Practice of Recruiting Americans in the U.S.A.
and Third World Countries*, stated, "In the U.S., in addition to ordinary cover, we use various international
organizations. The most important of these is the
United Nations and its branch institutions."[10]

Arkady N. Shevchenko served as under secretary
general of the United Nations when he defected in
1978. When he took the post as chief of the Security
Council and Political Affairs Division of the Soviet
Mission to the U.N., Shevchenko said he quickly
learned that most of his staffers worked for Soviet
intelligence services. "I had a staff of more than twenty
diplomats. I soon discovered that in fact there were
only seven who were real diplomats; the remainder
were KGB or GRU professionals under diplomatic
cover."[11]

Shevchenko said the Soviet government had a
practice of demanding "kickbacks" from the salaries
of Soviet nationals who worked at the U.N. In other
words, the Soviets were paid significantly less than
what their U.N. salaries dictated and the "excess" was
sent back to Moscow. Shevchenko explained:

> These kickbacks provided significant benefits
> for the Soviet Union. The Mission managed to
> cover almost all its expenses from the earnings
> of UN employees. The United States is the big
> loser in this, because it bears the heaviest fi-

nancial burden of contributions to the UN budget. To add insult to injury, at least half the Soviet nationals working in the international organization are not diplomats, but KGB or GRU professionals. Through the kickbacks, the United States indirectly finances the activity of Soviet intelligence services.[12]

The Soviets, Shevchenko explained, did not regard the U.N. as a forum to seriously debate issues. In describing work on an anti-American speech before the U.N. General Assembly to be delivered by Soviet foreign minister Andrei Gromyko, Shevchenko said:

> Working with Gromyko in the course of this exercise was enlightening. Certainly I knew that our leadership made every effort to utilize the United Nations in the interests of the Soviet Union and did not often act in consonance with the provisions of the UN Charter; other UN members conducted themselves in a similar war. But it was also clear that Gromyko, one of the UN's founding fathers, held a nihilistic, cynical, hypocritical view of the organization's activities and goals. He had come to regard it as no more than a forum for disseminating propaganda and abuse, ignoring it if the UN did anything out of line with Soviet policy and using it in situations where it profited Moscow or its clients.[13]

In the all-important post of U.N. secretariat, Shevchenko said the orders from Moscow were to "use or manipulate" it. He said his orders were to "prevent inclusion of anything detrimental to Soviet interests in Secretariat reports or studies, whether true or not," and make sure that "materials or conclusions favorable to the Soviet Union were included, also irrespective of the truth." He said the Soviets also found the Secretariat useful for collecting political and technical information.[14]

Another important activity was using the U.N. to assist the World Peace Council, a Soviet-front organization Shevchenko described as swarming with KGB officers. He said, "Moscow wanted to boost the Council's prestige by creating high-visibility via UN recognition of the Council's 'great role in the world movement for peace.' "[15]

Former KGB officers confirm that Soviet intelligence services used the U.N. as a major base and that this practice grew at a time of detente, when relations between the United States and the Soviet Union were supposed to be improving. Gordievsky wrote, "The size of the KGB presence in both the United States and the UN delegation in New York increased more rapidly at the height of detente than at any other period: from about 120 officers in 1970 to 220 in 1975."[16]

Oleg Kalugin, a former major general in the KGB, was a secret KGB agent when he was elected vice president of the United Nations Correspondents' Association. He said:

> Another transparent ruse in the espionage game was our so-called "U.N. Mission" in New York, which in fact was little more than a nest of KGB spies and intelligence officers. . . . The mission was headquarters to about three hundred Soviets, more than a third of whom were KGB officers.[17]

One of the early cases of Soviet espionage involving the U.N. concerned Valentine A. Gubitchev, a Soviet citizen employed by the body. He was observed by the FBI on 4 March 1949, holding a clandestine meeting with Judith Coplon, an employee of the U.S. Department of Justice. Herbert Romerstein, a U.S.

expert on Soviet espionage, and Stanislav Levchenko, a former KGB officer, describe what happened.

> They were arrested and searched. Coplon had in her purse summaries of confidential FBI reports on Soviet espionage. . . .
>
> The pair were convicted of espionage and sentenced to fifteen years in prison. Gubitchev had his sentence suspended as part of an agreement that he would leave the United States and never return. Coplon's conviction was overturned on technical grounds. She was freed and never retried.[18]

In some cases, Soviet manipulation and penetration of the U.N. became so obvious that the United States had to respond. Perhaps the most blatant example of this was the overt Soviet takeover of the U.N. Educational, Scientific, and Cultural Organization (UNESCO). In a 1985 speech, former Communist intelligence agent Ladislav Bittman described how UNESCO had become "an aggressively political institution, in which the Soviets constantly instigate radical Third world countries to take stands against Western standpoints and proposals."[19] However, this provoked a U.S. response; the Reagan administration withdrew from UNESCO in response to its anti-Americanism and corrupt practices.

But, the Soviets were using the U.N. in many other ways. In the late 1970s, for example, they launched a major "disarmament" campaign that attempted to use the U.N. in an effort to halt American nuclear weapons production and deployment of intermediate-range nuclear forces in Western Europe. American Pershing and Cruise missiles were being deployed to counter the threat posed by Soviet SS-20 missiles. In the United States, opposition to this deployment was called the "nuclear freeze" campaign. One of its goals was using the U.N. Special Session on Disarmament in June 1982 to embarrass the United States.

Notes from a meeting of the "bureau" of the presidential committee of the Soviet-front World Peace Council were extremely revealing and confirmed what defector Shevchenko said about the extremely close relationship that existed between the U.N. and the Soviets and their agents. In fact, Shevchenko was named in them.

> On January 30, 1978, at United Nations headquarters in New York, immediately after the Washington sessions had ended, the members of the Bureau held long and fruitful discussions with the Secretary General of the United Nations, Kurt Waldheim. . . .
>
> The United Nations Secretary General emphasized the great importance he attached to the role of the World Peace Council in creating the atmosphere for the success of the Special Session Devoted to Disarmament.
>
> A well-attended reception was held in honor of the Bureau at UN headquarters, hosted by Under-Secretary-General Arkady Shevchenko, who heads the UN division responsible for disarmament questions.[20]

Interestingly, a separate World Peace Council (WPC) document noted that it was "worth recalling" that an "initiative on general and complete disarmament" had been "unanimously" supported by the U.N. General Assembly as early as 1959. This was the document which led to an unprecedented Soviet-American agreement during the Kennedy administration calling for the dismantling of national armed forces and the establishment of a United Nations "peace force." The WPC hinted at this role for the U.N. by saying:

We expect the United Nations, whose aim is to maintain peace by promoting a system of lasting collective security in the world, to play an even more important role in this respect. . . . Being one of the contributors to the process of detente in the world, the UN itself undergoes a positive evolution and becomes an ever more significant element of the infrastructure of world security and peace.[21]

In 1981, as part of the process leading up to the U.N. disarmament session, the WPC applied for special "non-governmental" status with the U.N. Economic and Social Council, an important U.N. organ. In this case, however, the Soviets did not get their way. The United States objected on the grounds that the WPC was an organization whose funds almost certainly were derived from the Soviet government. The WPC application was withdrawn.[22]

But, this didn't stop Communist organizations and fronts from using the U.N. or manipulating domestic U.S. groups. The Soviet-funded Communist Party USA and CPUSA-front U.S. Peace Council were "actively involved" in the nuclear freeze campaign and were "among the organizers of the campaign's first national strategy conference in Washington, D.C. in March 1981." A Soviet KGB officer named Yuri Kapralov was also a participant.[23]

According to Edward J. O'Malley, assistant director for intelligence for the FBI, Soviet intelligence agents based at the U.N. played key roles in these activities of the CPUSA.

Several Soviet officials affiliated with the KGB at the Soviet Embassy in Washington, D.C., and the Soviet Mission to the United Nations are in regular contact with CPUSA members and officials of CPUSA front groups. They monitor CPUSA activities and transmit guidance to the CPUSA officials.[24]

The Soviet fronts were also involved in "infiltrating and influencing" a group called the June 12 Committee, which planned and coordinated demonstrations on American soil during the U.N. disarmament event. CPUSA official Sandra Pollock, a leader of the U.S. Peace Council, was on the June 12 executive committee.[25] The purpose of the demonstrations was to create the perception that there was overwhelming public sentiment against the U.S. nuclear weapons program and to stop the deployment of such weapons in Western Europe, even while the Soviets continued building and deploying their own.

At the time, these intelligence and propaganda activities were extremely effective. President Reagan even felt compelled to attend the U.N. disarmament conference, where he delivered a speech urging improvement in U.S.-Soviet relations.

However, in his autobiography, *An American Life*, the true feelings of disdain that President Reagan had about the U.N. came through in a section dealing with the U.N.'s role in the Cold War. In 1986, after the U.S. arrested a Soviet spy in the U.S, Soviet KGB agents seized and imprisoned a Moscow correspondent for *U.S. News & World Report*, Nicholas Daniloff, and accused him of spying for the United States. The trumped-up charges against Daniloff angered Reagan, who recognized the arrest of Daniloff as a typical Soviet ploy to grab an innocent American and then offer him in exchange for the apprehended Soviet agent.

In retaliation, in a September 9 entry in his personal diary, Reagan proposed that we "kick a half hundred of their UN KGB agents out of the country." The number, though, dwindled down to twenty-five. "We're sending 25 of their UN staff home," Reagan wrote. "All are KGB agents." When the secretary general of the U.N. stated that the U.S. eviction of the Soviets was against the U.N. charter Reagan commented, "He'd better be careful, if we cut off [their] UN allowance they might be out of business."[26]

Reagan's reaction reflects the fact that, during the Cold War, the U.N. was essentially on the Communist side. If Reagan had not been influenced by advisers such as Secretary of State George Shultz, who mainly handled the Daniloff affair, he might have followed through on his instincts and tried to cut off U.S. assistance to the world body.

John R. Bolton, assistant secretary of state for international organization affairs during the Bush administration, points out that the U.N. failed to play a positive role in "the most profound and dangerous regional standoff" during the forty years of the Cold War—the division of Europe. "There," Bolton said, "NATO prevailed, the Warsaw Pact collapsed and the U.N. was missing in action."

Bolton also points out that modern-day U.N. "successes" invariably turn out to be peacekeeping operations in countries of the world—Namibia, Cambodia, El Salvador and Mozambique—where Communist proxies or client states instigated the warfare. The U.N. intervened in these areas, Bolton pointed out, only after the Cold War receded.[27] Another example of this phenomenon is Angola, where a Soviet client state waged war on anti-Communist guerrillas. The U.N. Security Council voted in February 1995 to send seven thousand peacekeepers to the country to monitor a ceasefire there.

One of the worst performances turned in by the U.N. during the Cold War was its failure to hold the Soviets accountable for violations of international agreements outlawing chemical and biological weapons. In 1979, there was a release of spores from a Soviet biological warfare plant in Sverdlovsk that killed several dozen people. The Soviets lied, saying the outbreak was a natural one originating in tainted meat. The U.N. accepted these ridiculous Soviet denials.

President Reagan, in a speech to the U.N., himself accused the Soviets and their clients of using chemical or biological weapons called "yellow rain" in Southeast Asia and Afghanistan during the early 1980s. The Soviets naturally denied the charges and the U.N. accepted the denials, although the world body did confirm Iraq's use of chemical/biological weapons in a 1984 attack on Iran. However, conveniently for the Soviets, the U.N. never traced the Iraqi program to Moscow.

In the critical Middle East, a source of much of our domestic oil, both the U.N. and Moscow have played an insidious game. After World War II, in which millions of Jews were murdered under Nazi tyranny, the U.N. created a home for Jews in Palestine with the approval of the United States and the Soviet Union. The U.N. General Assembly in 1947 voted to partition Palestine into Arab and Jewish states, but the Arabs rejected the plan and waged war after Israel declared itself a state in 1948. The Arabs lost this war, as well as wars against Israel which followed in 1967 and 1973.

Meanwhile, under Arab sponsorship, the Palestine Liberation Organization (PLO) was formed to liberate Palestine from Israel and established very close ties to Moscow.

The U.N. came down on the side of tne PLO, giving the group observer status and permitting PLO chairman Yasser Arafat, wearing a side-arm on his hip, to address the General Assembly in New York in 1974. The full extent of U.N. support for Arafat's PLO was documented in the book, *A Mandate for Terror:*

The United Nations and the PLO.[28] The author, Harris
O. Schoenberg, said the U.N.'s embrace of the PLO,
in light of its record of terrorism, made a mockery of
the world's body self-proclaimed opposition to terrorism. Analyst Christopher Story argues that the U.N. in
fact "sustained" the PLO over the years through a
host of U.N. agencies and programs, and that since
the main contributor to the U.N. has always been the
United States, the world body became a "conduit for
the diversion of U.S. taxpayers' money" to the group.[29]

With the weight of the U.N. against it, the Israeli
government announced an accord with the PLO in
1993, dramatized when Israeli Prime Minister Yitzhak
Rabin shook hands on the White House lawn with
Arafat at a ceremony presided over by President
Clinton. Many observers, including supporters of Israel, believe the agreement will inevitably lead to the
establishment of a PLO state with continued close ties
to Moscow.

"Not surprisingly," writes Story,

> Arafat and other PLO leaders have been clam-
> oring since early 1990 for United Nations
> "peacekeeping troops" to protect a new PLO
> state in the West Bank and Gaza. The Clinton
> Administration soon joined in this chorus . . .
> Israel Radio said that Victor Posuyalyuk,
> Russia's Special envoy to the Middle East, had
> commented that his country was "very inter-
> ested in being part of an international pres-
> ence" [in the region].[30]

A similar outcome was forecast by former Kennedy
official Richard Gardner in a *Foreign Affairs* article
titled "The Hard Road To World Order." He wrote:

> The Soviet union, China and the United States
> may be unable to agree on the general rules
> that should cover U.N. peacekeeping in all un-

specified future contingencies, but they may well agree on a U.N. peacekeeping force to secure a permanent Middle East settlement that is otherwise satisfactory to them.[31]

Some might argue that, with the collapse of Soviet-style communism, the U.N. and Moscow can truly play a constructive role in the Middle East and elsewhere. However, the circumstances under which Soviet-style communism collapsed have to be completely understood in order to grasp what kind of a role the U.N. and Russia may be playing right now.

The case of Aldrich Ames clearly demonstrates that whether they call themselves Soviets or Russians, Communists or former Communists, their intelligence activities against the United States continue. Ames, a high-ranking CIA official, started working for the Soviets in 1985 and continued working for the Russians after the Soviet Union collapsed through 1994, when he was arrested and convicted of espionage.

The Ames case raises questions about the nature of the changes which have taken place in the old Soviet Union. Anatoliy Golitsyn, the ex-KGB agent who wrote the book, *New Lies for Old*, forecasting "false liberalization" in Eastern Europe and the Soviet Union, argues in his new book, *The Perestroika Deception*, that Soviet President Mikhail Gorbachev's policy of "perestroika" or the restructuring of Soviet society was part of a strategic plan to fool the West into thinking authentic changes were taking place in the Soviet Union. Golitsyn says the Soviet Communists believed that, in order for them to continue to pursue their goal of world communism, it was necessary to convince the West they had made an irrevocable "break with the past." They did this, he argues, through the deceptive "suspension" of the Communist party.

Other experts look at the situation differently. Dr.

John Lenczowski, former director of European and
Soviet Affairs at the National Security Council, and
Dr. J. Michael Waller, author of *Secret Empire*, contend
that some of Gorbachev's reforms were authentic but
that they went out of control, leading to the unin-
tended disintegration of the Communist party and the
Soviet Union. Waller agrees, though, that Gorbachev
never intended to weaken the KGB. On the contrary:

> His was a conscious policy to strengthen the
> KGB while attempting to create the conditions
> for Soviet society to become more creative and
> dynamic under the continued guidance and
> regulation of the Communist Party of the So-
> viet Union.[32]

Much may never be known about the major events
before, during and after the fall of the Soviet Union.
Peter Schweizer's book, *Victory*, argues strongly that
the Reagan administration had a secret strategy involving the Vatican that hastened the collapse of the
Soviet Union. Discussing a series of communications
between the Vatican and Reagan CIA Director William Casey, which produced a "willingness to cooper-
ate" between the two sides, Schweizer reported, "The
assassination attempt on the pope and the declaration
of martial law [in his native Poland by the Soviet puppet
regime] had affected him deeply."[33]

Claire Sterling documents in her book, *The Time
of the Assassins*, how the attempt on the life of the pope
led to a Bulgarian connection and, beyond that, to the
Soviet KGB itself.[34] The pope had to be aware of this.

A chapter in Pope John Paul II's own book, *Crossing the Threshold of Hope*, deals with the sensational
topic, "Was God at Work in the Fall of Communism?"
During his first visit to formerly Soviet-occupied territory, the pope suggested that the *digitus Dei* or "finger
of God" could be discerned in the collapse of Soviet

communism. He called it a "mystery," even a "miracle."
But, the pope did not say with certainty what he
thought had really happened. While declaring that "in
the fall of communism the action of God has become
almost visible in history," he also said, "it would be
simplistic to say that Divine Providence caused the fall
of Communism."

Regardless of how and why the changes occurred,
analyst Story, the editor of Golitsyn's second book,
argues persuasively that both Russian President Boris
Yeltsin and his predecessor Mikhail Gorbachev are
still committed to a one world government, which
they intend to be dominated by Communists, and that
the U.N. is seen by them an instrument for the fur-
therance of this objective.

The fact that Yeltsin is dominated by the old Soviet military and the KGB is demonstrated by his failure to expose and shutdown the ongoing Russian
chemical/biological weapons program. This program
was the subject of a major investigative piece by J.
Michael Waller in the October 1994 *Reader's Digest.*
Assuming he is sober, there is no question that Yeltsin
knows what is going on. Indeed, he was the chief
Communist party official in Sverdlovsk at the time of
the 1979 incident.

A U.S. congressional hearing which exposed the
Sverdlovsk incident as the result of biological warfare
research was held on 29 May 1980. The congressman
who presided over the hearing was Les Aspin, who
became Clinton's defense secretary.[37] After the Persian Gulf War, Aspin initiated a furious Pentagon effort
to develop defenses against biological warfare agents,
even while denying they were used on our troops in
the Gulf.

As Russian president, Yeltsin finally came clean
about the Sverdlovsk incident in a 1992 speech, ac-

knowledging, "The KGB admitted that our military developments were the cause."[38] The problem is that Yeltsin only seems able to "admit" what the KGB authorizes him to.

This author subsequently tried to link the Russian program to the health problems known as Gulf War Syndrome afflicting as many as fifty thousand American veterans of the Persian Gulf War. There is evidence that chemical or biological weapons were used on our troops by Iraq and that they may have been supplied by Moscow, possibly through the PLO.[39] Authors Joseph Douglass, Jr., and Neil C. Livingstone have argued that chemical/biological agents were provided to Iraq when the Arabs, concerned about Israel's nuclear weapons capability, demanded weapons of mass destruction in response. The Arabs, though, had wanted *nuclear* weapons.

The irony is that while President Reagan's military buildup and Strategic Defense Initiative (SDI) were seen by some conservatives as pivotal in the Soviet decline, the Soviets/Russians may have developed a more devastating weapon that could end up destroying the West and may even now be serving as a form of blackmail against our policy makers. Russian dissidents have identified this new class of poisons as "Novichok" or newcomer.

A further irony is that the Soviets were developing their stockpile of chemical and biological weapons while they were engaging in a worldwide disinformation campaign accusing the Pentagon of creating the AIDS virus at a military laboratory. In fact, it may be the Soviets/Russians/Cubans who are spreading these diseases, including AIDS and a possibly related illness, Chronic Fatigue Immune Dysfunction Syndrome (CFIDS). The Pentagon's Defense Science Board has itself reported that Gulf War Syndrome is similar to CFIDS.

Some contend the Clinton administration is not publicly acknowledging that chemical or biological agents were used in the Persian Gulf War because it would lead to paying billions of dollars in health benefits to sick veterans. But, this doesn't make much sense, especially in view of the fact that the Clinton administration was more than willing to spend billions of dollars on a government-run health care system. Another explanation is that the cover-up stems from the likelihood that admitting a Russian connection to the problem could embarrass Yeltsin and return our two countries to Cold War tensions.

Despite the controversy over Gulf War Syndrome, the Persian Gulf War is still cited as an example of how the Soviets cooperated with the United States in this era of "new thinking." Gorbachev, after all, was said to have "cooperated" with the United States and the U.N. in approving military action against Iraq, a Soviet client state.

"Moscow's reasoning was too subtle for the West to understand," Christopher Story explains. By "cooperating" with the West, he maintains, Moscow "convinced the whole world that the confrontation between East and West was over for good, thereby laying the foundation for the next stage of their offensive against the West."

Indeed, it didn't take long for the Russians to demonstrate they were going to use the U.N. on behalf of their own interests and those of their friends. As noted by Sen. Bob Dole, a strong critic of Clinton's "Russia-first" policy, the first substantive U.N. Security Council veto exercised by Russia since 1984 (during the Cold War) came in December 1994 on the issue of tougher sanctions against Serbia.

As for former Soviet President Gorbachev, who says he is now involved in a "different political role," he has openly taken up the cause of strengthening the U.N. Story explains:

> Former Soviet President Gorbachev set out Moscow's agenda, in which the United Nations plays a part, both in his "end of the Cold War" speech at Fulton, Missouri, in May 1992, and in his Nobel Peace Prize speech in the following month. Both speeches contained proposals which gravely threaten the West.
>
> For instance, Gorbachev spoke of "limitations" to national sovereignty, in cases where the international community deems that human rights abuses are taking place. The purpose of this notion is to erode the integrity of national borders. A second theme he floated was the use of force [should be] formally restricted to "the international community," which means that the use of force by nation-states acting alone or in concert is precluded.
>
> Once an international structure is the sole legitimate user of military power, we have the framework for a de facto global dictatorship.[40]

Gorbachev has concentrated many of his activities in the United States. In January of 1992, he established the International Foundation for Socio-Economic and Political Studies in Moscow, known as the Gorbachev Foundation, while a Gorbachev Foundation/USA was established in the United States at the same time. The objectives were said to be:

> Fostering international debate and cooperation on the vital contemporary issues confronting humanity; providing humanitarian assistance to those adversely affected by political and social turbulence in the former Soviet bloc; redefining global security in a rapidly changing world; and promoting sustainable uses of the world's

resources and mitigating devastating human impact on our fragile environment.

A brochure for the Gorbachev Foundation identified the chairman of the board of directors as former Sen. Alan Cranston of California and the chairman of the advisory board as former Reagan Secretary of State George Shultz. The selection of Cranston is significant. As an official of the U.S. Office of War Information in 1943, he was accused of trying to intimidate Polish-language radio stations in the United States which highlighted the Soviet murder of thousands of Polish officers during the war. At the time, the United States was allied with the Soviets against the Nazis, who discovered the massacre. In their book on Soviet espionage operations, Romerstein and Levchenko say about Cranston's actions, "It's hard to tell whether this was overzealous patriotism, but it served a Soviet purpose in covering up a Soviet atrocity." They also reported that, "Cranston admitted that he had hired David Karr, although he knew Karr had written articles for the [Communist] *Daily Worker*. Cranston claimed he did not know that Karr was a member of the Communist Party."[41]

One of the objectives of the Gorbachev Foundation—promoting "sustainable" development—also happens to be a key goal of the U.N. The concept involves government-imposed limits to economic growth. At the 1992 U.N.-sponsored Earth Summit, an Earth Charter was presented to regulate industrial development on a worldwide basis under U.N auspices.

As president of Green Cross International, an environmental group, Gorbachev delivered the 17 October 1994, keynote address at the annual awards dinner of the Hollywood-funded Environmental Media Association. Gorbachev spoke to over seven hundred members of the entertainment community about the need for a "universally binding international code of environmental ethics," saying, "There must be a kind of ten commandments for the environment, something that no one would be allowed to violate." Gorbachev added that "developing international environmental law" was a goal of his Green Cross group.

In this case, however, it won't be God who enforces the law. Apparently, the enforcer will be the United Nations or even a world government. Gorbachev declared, "We have joined forces with the Earth Council... to draft such a code, and I hope that its guidelines will be presented to the conference marking the 50th anniversary of the United Nations."[42]

The irony is that Gorbachev presided over probably the most environmentally irresponsible nation in human history. The 1992 book, *Ecocide in the USSR*, describing the environmental and medical crisis in the former Soviet Union, said, "No other great industrial civilization so systematically and so long poisoned its land, air, water and people. None so loudly proclaiming its efforts to improve public health and protect nature, so degraded both."[43] Gorbachev's answer to this problem on a worldwide basis—a code of conduct enforced by some international body—is a prescription for even more disaster. He still doesn't recognize—or pretends not to grasp—that a central government bureaucracy cannot effectively regulate the environment. But, his comments are understandable in the context of laying the groundwork for a world government.

During 27 September–1 October 1995, the Gorbachev Foundation is scheduled to host a State of the World Forum in San Francisco, California, at which Gorbachev and Maurice Strong, who served as secretary-general of the U.N.'s Earth Summit, are intending to present a new version of the Earth Charter. Participants are to include former British Prime Minister

Margaret Thatcher, former President George Bush, George Shultz, broadcaster Ted Turner, and futurist John Naisbitt.

But, Dr. Malachi Martin, the Vatican insider, says the pope is not fooled by Gorbachev. He says the pope regards Gorbachev as a follower of Antonio Gramsci, an Italian Communist who taught that communism would succeed in the West not through violent revolution but through "infiltration" of cultural institutions. Martin writes that liberation theology, an attempt to peddle Marxism using Christian words and phrases, is a "faithful exercise of Gramsci's principles."

Martin, whose book, *The Keys of This Blood*, examines what he views as a struggle for world dominion between spiritual and secular forces, says about Gorbachev and the pope:

> There are still many questions to answer about Mikhail Gorbachev; and it may be that Gorbachev himself cannot yet answer even some of the most important ones. But about his secularist stance there is no doubt in Pope John Paul's mind. The man behind the outstretched hand is a master of Antonio Gramsci's technique of cultural penetration. Following the edicts of Gramsci, he has clearly recognized the seductive value of secularism among democratic capitalists. As the direct heir to Lenin, and the first of his successors to abandon the Stalinist distortions of Leninism, Gorbachev has at last successfully presented Leninism to the West. And he has done so in respectable—not to say dazzling—secularist terms.[44]

But, cultural penetration—or convergence, as Golitsyn prefers to call it—proceeds on several fronts, official and unofficial. Since the collapse of the Soviet Communist system, the Russians have initiated certain forms of "mutual cooperation" with Western intelligence and military services. J. Michael Waller noted that, at a Moscow conference on a Transformed Russia in the New World, Yevgeni Primakov, chief of Russian foreign intelligence

> gave a familiar list of mutual interests: "nonproliferation of vital technologies, combatting terrorism, and preventing regional conflicts from developing into global crises." Counternarcotics was another favored subject of mutual cooperation that led to conferences with officials of Western secret services. Curiously, a CIA delegate to a joint 1991 conference on fighting drug trafficking was none other than Aldrich Ames.[45]

The irony is that, as Waller points out, Primakov, a holdover from the old Soviet era, was "an architect of Soviet support for international terrorism against the West in the West in the 1970s and '80s. Now he is calling for cooperation with the West in the 'struggle against terrorism,' without granting Western intelligence services complete access to the KGB terrorist files."[46]

The same point can be made in relation to offers of Russian "cooperation" in fighting illegal drugs. Primakov could help by telling Western intelligence officials all he knows about the Communist role in international drug trafficking. In his book, *Red Cocaine*, Joseph Douglass, Jr., documented the role of the Soviet Union and other Communist powers, including Cuba, in the drug problem afflicting the West. The purpose of the Communist campaign was not only to demoralize the West but raise hard currency and identify drug users who could be blackmailed for intelligence purposes.[47]

One writer, Mark Almond, has speculated that

Ames' role in U.S. anti-drug efforts may help explain why U.S. officials tended to pooh-pooh reports of Soviet and Cuban involvement in the drug trade in the 1980s. Ames, in other words, was feeding the CIA disinformation about the Communist role and telling the Soviets what we knew.[48]

However, rather than expose the Communist role in terrorism, drug trafficking, and other evils, the U.N. is now focusing its attention on "international organized crime," including something it calls the Russian Mafia, which supposedly has no links to the Russian government. In April of 1995, the U.N. was scheduled to host a "crime conference" in Cairo, where American and Russian delegates were going to plot strategy together. Waller has commented that "such cooperation is fraught with dangers" because, "Russia's organized criminals are not only rogue elements battling the authorities. In many, many instances, they are the authorities themselves."[49]

In 1994, President Clinton's FBI director, Louis J. Freeh, announced a high-profile effort to work with Russian services in fighting organized crime. However, after getting briefed on official government links to "Russian organized crime," Freeh changed course somewhat, declaring that the bureau will only work with Russians "of integrity, who are committed to democratic law enforcement."

But, the most astonishing cases of U.S.-Russian "cooperation" have occurred in the military field, with the U.N. destined to play a key role once again.

In 1993, at a summit in Vancouver, President Clinton and Russian President Boris Yeltsin announced the establishment of a "strategic partnership" between the two countries that involved military cooperation. At the conclusion of a September 8 Pentagon ceremony, where a Memorandum of Understanding was signed by then-Defense Secretary Les Aspin and Russian Defense Minister Pavel Grachev, Aspin said that, "Following President Clinton's direction, I have made building this partnership a top priority." He said, "It is a partnership in which military and defense relations play a leading role."[50]

Aspin explained:

> It is an agreement that recognizes that the well-being and the security of the United States and the Russian Federation are vitally related. It is an agreement that seeks to put the years of superpower rivalry and nuclear confrontation behind us. And it is an agreement that builds for the future by formally establishing a series of continuing contacts and relationships between our two defense establishments.[51]

The initiatives in the memorandum included a peacekeeping exercise involving military forces from both countries. The exercise, dubbed "Peacekeeping 94" and featuring 250 U.S. and 250 Russian infantry soldiers, was carried out in September of 1994 in Russia. The Americans used Russian helicopters and armored personnel carriers because they were not allowed to bring their own equipment. A bigger joint exercise is planned for this year in the United States.[52]

Significantly, the idea of U.S.-Russian peacekeeping exercises was an idea proposed by Grachev. The *Washington Post* even reported, "One official said Aspin welcomed the idea enthusiastically, adding that there is a real prospect that Russians or Americans might operate one day under the command of their former chief adversary."[53]

How might U.S. forces be commanded by Russians? The U.N. provides the answer.

President Clinton's "Policy on Reforming Multilateral Peace Operations," a document on U.S. involvement in U.N. peacekeeping, included this curious paragraph: "With respect to the question of peacekeeping in the territory of the former Soviet Union, requests for traditional UN blue-helmeted operations will be considered on the same basis as other requests."[54]

An analysis of this document noted that the use of the phrase "territory of the former Soviet Union" implied an Eastern Europe "still defined in terms of Russian imperialism rather than by the establishment of independent states."[55] It suggested that U.N. troops could be deployed at Russia's request to reassert Russian control over the "former" Soviet Union.

It didn't take long until a version of this came to pass. On 22 July 1994, the U.N. Security Council approved a resolution "welcoming Russia's contribution to a peacekeeping force in Abkhazia," a region of Georgia. The Russian ambassador to the U.N., Yuli Vorontsov, had said that without U.N. acceptance of Russian peacekeeping in Georgia, Moscow would veto a U.N. resolution authorizing an invasion of Haiti. *Washington Post* foreign affairs columnist Lally Weymouth called it a "cynical deal," noting that "the United States has given Russia the right to reoccupy the Caucasus and other former Soviet republics in return for Russian acquiescence in U.N. Security Council resolutions on Haiti." But, Weymouth also saw the whole exercise as a violation of the U.N.'s own rules.

> In supporting, albeit tacitly, Russian "peacekeeping" in Georgia, the United States appears to have redefined the U.N. peace-keeping mandate. For example, under the U.N. Charter, no more than one-third of a peace-keeping force can come from any one country. But the "peacekeepers" in Georgia are almost exclusively Russian.[56]

With the Clinton administration in power—and a timid Republican Congress—it seems as if it is just a matter of time before U.S. and Russian troops, with U.N. backing and assistance, are deployed together as members of a peacekeeping force that will stamp out cases of alleged human rights abuses. Supporters of the U.N. will be ecstatic, declaring that the United States and Russia will have laid the groundwork for a U.N.-sponsored "world army" that will maintain lasting peace, perhaps as part of a world government. And, the prospect of American troops being commanded by Russian military officers will almost certainly come to pass.

Notes

1. Herbert Romerstein and Stanislav Levchenko, *The KGB Against the 'Main Enemy'* (Lexington, Massachusetts: Lexington Books, 1989), 214.

2. Anatoliy Golitsyn, *New Lies for Old* (New York: Dodd, Mead & Company, 1984), 69.

3. Christopher Andrew and Oleg Gordievsky, *KGB: The Inside Story* (New York: HarperCollins Publishers, 1990): 332–340.

4. Gordievsky, *KGB*, 338–339.

5. See Maj. Gen. John K. Singlaub and Malcolm McConnell, *Hazardous Duty* (New York: Summit Books, 1991), 365.

6. Gus Constantine, "Did Stalin Give OK for Kim Il-Sung's Attack on S. Korea?" *Washington Times* (24 February 1995): A16.

7. Singlaub, *Hazardous*, 180.

8. Raymond S. Sleeper, *A Lexicon of Marxist-Leninist Semantics*, ed. (Alexandria, Virginia: Western Goals, 1983), 305.

9. *Contemporary Soviet Propaganda and Disinformation: A Conference Report*, United States Department of State, Department of State Publication 9536, Released March 1987.

10. John Barron, *KGB: The Secret Work of Soviet Secret Agents* (New York: Bantam Books, Inc., 1974), 24.

11. Arkady N. Shevchenko, *Breaking With Moscow* (New York: Alfred A. Knopf, 1985), 313.

12. Ibid., 132.

13. Ibid., 161.

14. Ibid., 225.

15. Ibid.

16. Gordievsky, *KGB*, 540.

17. Oleg Kalugin, *The First Directorate: My 32 Years in Intelligence and Espionage Against the West* (New York: St. Martin's Press, 1994), 34–35.

18. Romerstein and Levchenko, *The KGB Against*, 243.

19. *Contemporary Soviet Propaganda and Disinformation*, 114.

20. "WPC Call from Washington, D.C. WPC Bureau Meeting. International Dialogue for Disarmament and Detente, Washington, D.C. January 25–28, 1978," *Soviet Active Measures*, Hearings Before the Permanent Select Committee on Intelligence, House of Representatives, 13, 14 July 1982. (U.S. Government Printing Office, Washington: 1982), 241.

21. Ibid., 267.

22. Richard H. Shultz and Roy Godson, *Dezinformatsia: Active Measures in Soviet Strategy* (Washington, D.C.: Pergamon-Brassey's, 1984), 119.

23. Ibid., 117.

24. *Soviet Active Measures*, 203.

25. Shultz and Godson, *Dezinformatsia*, 118.

26. Ronald Reagan, *An American Life* (New York: Simon and Schuster, 1990), 668.

27. John R. Bolton, "Dulles Would Disagree," *Washington Post* (6 March 1995): A17.

28. Harris O. Schoenberg, *A Mandate for Terror: The United Nations and the PLO* (New York: Shapolsky Publishers, Inc., 1989).

29. Christopher Story, "The False Peace in the Middle East," *International Currency Review* (Autumn 1994): 69.

30. Ibid., 70.

31. Richard N. Gardner, "The Hard Road to World Order," *Foreign Affairs* (April 1974): 563.

32. J. Michael Waller, *Secret Empire: The KGB in Russia Today* (Boulder, Colorado: Westview Press, 1994), 2.

33. Peter Schweizer, *Victory* (New York: The Atlantic Monthly Press, 1994), 70.

34. See Claire Sterling, *The Time of the Assassins* (New York: Hole, Rinehart and Winston, 1983).

35. John Paul II, *Crossing the Threshold of Hope* (New York: Alfred A. Knopf, Inc., 1994), 130-131.

36. Ibid., 131-132.

37. The Sverdlovsk Incident: Soviet Compliance with the Biological Weapons Convention. Hearing Before the Subcommittee on Oversight of the Permanent Select Committee on Intelligence, House of Representatives, 29 May 29 1980.

38. Philip J. Hilts, "'79 Soviet Anthrax Outbreak Linked to Biological War Plant," *New York Times* (18 November 1994): A26.

39. Cliff Kincaid, "Russia's Dirty Chemical Secret," *The American Legion Magazine* (February 1995).

40. "U.S. Taxpayers Fund Russian Expansion," *The Free American* (Freedom Alliance), September 1994.

41. Romerstein and Levchenko, *The KGB Against*, 228.

42. "Mikhail Gorbachev Addresses Fourth Annual environmental Media Awards," *Green Light*, vol. 5, iss. 5 (November/December 1994), Environmental Media Association.

43. Murray Feshbach and Alfred Friendly, Jr., *Ecocide in the USSR* (New York: Basic Books, 1992), 1.

44. Malachi Martin, *The Keys of This Blood: The Struggle for World Dominion Between Pope John Paul II, Mikhail Gorbachev & The Capitalist West* (New York: Simon & Schuster, 1990), 363.

45. Waller, *Secret Empire*, 268.

46. J. Michael Waller, "The KGB Isn't Dead Yet," *The Wall Street Journal Europe* (28 January 1992).

47. See Joseph D. Douglass, Jr., *Red Cocaine, The Drugging of America* (Atlanta: Clarion House, Inc., 1990).

48. Mark Almond, "The KGB and America's War on Drugs," *The Wall Street Journal* (10 March 1994).

49. J. Michael Waller, "Russia's Biggest 'Mafia' Is the KGB," *The Wall Street Journal Europe* (22 June 1994).

50. Media Availability with Les Aspin, U.S. Secretary of Defense, and General of the Army Pavel Grachev, Russian Minister of Defense, The Pentagon, Arlington, Virginia, Defense Department Briefing, 8 September 1993.

51. Ibid.

52. Steve Vogel, "Joint Drill in Russia," *Army Times* (19 September 1994): 6.

53. Barton Gellman, "Brothers-in Arms: Now GI Joe and Ivan to Train Together," *Washington Post* (9 September 1993): A1.

54. Quoted in "Clinton's U.N. Peacekeeping Plan Still Flawed," Republican Research Committee, undated, 3.

55. Ibid.

56. Lally Weymouth, "Yalta II," *Washington Post* (24 July 1994): C7.

We welcome comments from our readers. Feel free to write to us at the following address:

Editorial Department
Huntington House Publishers
P.O. Box 53788
Lafayette, LA 70505

======

More Good Books from Huntington House

The Best of HUMAN EVENTS
Fifty Years of Conservative
Thought and Action
Edited by James C. Roberts

Before Ronald Reagan, before Barry Goldwater, since the closing days of World War II, HUMAN EVENTS stood against the prevailing winds of the liberal political Zeitgeist. HUMAN EVENTS has published the best of three generations of conservative writers—academics, journalists, philosophers, politicians: Frank Chodorov and Richard Weaver, Henry Hazlitt and Hans Sennholz, William F. Buckley and M. Stanton Evans, Jack Kemp and Dan Quayle. A representative sample of their work, marking fifty years of American political and social history, is here collected in a single volume.

ISBN 1-56384-018-9 $34.95 Hardback

Can Families Survive in Pagan America?
by Samuel Dresner

Drug addiction, child abuse, divorce, and the welfare state have dealt terrible, pounding blows to the family structure. At the same time, robbery, homicide, and violent assaults have increased at terrifying rates. But, according to the author, we can restore order to our country and our lives. Using the tenets of Jewish family life and faith, Dr. Dresner calls on Americans from every religion and walk of life to band together and make strong, traditional families a personal and national priority again—before it's too late.

ISBN Trade Paper: 1-56384-080-4 $15.99
Hardcover: 1-56384-086-3 $31.99

The Assault: Liberalism's Attack on Religion, Freedom, and Democracy
by Dale A. Berryhill

In *The Liberal Contradiction,* Berryhill showed just how ludicrous it is when civil rights advocates are racists and feminists are sexists. Now he turns to much more disturbing phenomena, revisiting such issues as censorship, civil rights, gay rights, and political correctness in education and offering commentary and punishment, civil liberties, multiculturalism, and religious freedom. Fortunately, the American people are catching on to the hypocrisy. Still, the culture war is far from over.

ISBN 1-56384-077-4 $9.99

How to Homeschool (Yes, You!)
by Julia Toto

Have you considered homeschooling for your children, but you just don't know where to begin? This book is the answer to your prayer. It will cover topics, such as; what's the best curriculum for your children; where to find the right books; if certified teachers teach better than stay-at-home moms; and what to tell your mother-in-law.

ISBN 1-56384-059-6 $4.99

Political Correctness: The Cloning of the American Mind
by David Thibodaux, Ph.D.

The author, a professor of literature at the University of Southwestern Louisiana, confronts head on the movement that is now being called Political Correctness. Political correctness, says Thibodaux, "is an umbrella under which advocates of civil rights, gay and lesbian rights, feminism, and environmental causes have gathered." To incur the wrath of these groups, one only has to disagree with them on political, moral, or social issues. To express traditionally Western concepts in universities today can result in not only ostracism, but even suspension. (According to a recent "McNeil-Lehrer News Hour" report, one student was suspended for discussing the reality of the moral law with an avowed homosexual. He was reinstated only after he apologized.)

ISBN 1-56384-026-X Trade Paper $9.99

Beyond Political Correctness: Are There Limits to This Lunacy?
by David Thibodaux

Author of the best-selling *Political Correctness: The Cloning of the American Mind,* Dr. David Thibodaux now presents his long awaited sequel—*Beyond Political Correctness: Are There Limits to This Lunacy?* The politically correct movement has now moved beyond college campuses. The movement has succeeded in turning the educational system of this country into a system of indoctrination. Its effect on education was predictable: steadily declining scores on every conceivable test which measures student performance; and, increasing numbers of college freshmen who know a great deal about condoms, homosexuality, and abortion, but whose basic skills in language, math, and science are alarmingly deficient.

ISBN 1-56384-066-9 $9.99

Order These Huntington House Books !

- America Betrayed—Marlin Maddoux. 7.99
- The Assault—Dale A. Berryhill 9.99
- Beyond Political Correctness—David Thibodaux 9.99
- The Best of HUMAN EVENTS—Edited by James C. Roberts 34.95
- Bleeding Hearts and Propaganda—James R. Spencer 9.99
- Can Families Survive in Pagan America?—Samuel Dresner 15.99
- Circle of Death—Richmond Odom 10.99
- Combat Ready—Lynn Stanley 9.99
- Conservative, American & Jewish—Jacob Neusner 9.99
- The Dark Side of Freemasonry—Ed Decker 9.99
- The Demonic Roots of Globalism—Gary Kah 10.99
- Don't Touch That Dial—Barbara Hattemer & Robert Showers ..... 9.99/19.99 HB
- En Route to Global Occupation—Gary Kah 9.99
- Everyday Evangelism—Ray Comfort 10.99
- *Exposing the AIDS Scandal—Dr. Paul Cameron 7.99/2.99
- Freud's War with God—Jack Wright, Jr. 7.99
- Gays & Guns—John Eidsmoe .... 7.99/14.99 HB
- Global Bondage—Cliff Kincaid 10.99
- Goddess Earth—Samantha Smith 9.99
- Health Begins in Him—Terry Dorian 9.99
- Heresy Hunters—Jim Spencer 8.99
- Hidden Dangers of the Rainbow—Constance Cumbey 9.99
- High-Voltage Christianity—Michael Brown 10.99
- High on Adventure—Stephen Arrington 8.99
- Homeless in America—Jeremy Reynalds 9.99
- How to Homeschool (Yes, You!)—Julia Toto 3.99
- Hungry for God—Larry E. Myers 9.99
- I Shot an Elephant in My Pajamas—Morrie Ryskind w/ John Roberts 12.99
- *Inside the New Age Nightmare—Randall Baer 9.99/2.99
- A Jewish Conservative Looks at Pagan America—Don Feder ..... 9.99/19.99 HB
- Journey into Darkness—Stephen Arrington 9.99
- Kinsey, Sex and Fraud—Dr. Judith A. Reisman & Edward Eichel 11.99
- The Liberal Contradiction—Dale A. Berryhill 9.99
- Legalized Gambling—John Eidsmoe 7.99
- Loyal Opposition—John Eidsmoe 8.99
- The Media Hates Conservatives—Dale A. Berryhill .... 9.99/19.99 HB
- New Gods for a New Age—Richmond Odom 9.99
- One Man, One Woman, One Lifetime—Rabbi Reuven Bulka 7.99
- Out of Control—Brenda Scott .... 9.99/19.99 HB
- Outcome-Based Education—Peg Luksik & Pamela Hoffecker 9.99
- The Parched Soul of America—Leslie Kay Hedger w/ Dave Reagan 10.99
- Please Tell Me—Tom McKenney 9.99
- Political Correctness—David Thibodaux 9.99
- Resurrecting the Third Reich—Richard Terrell 9.99
- Revival: Its Principles and Personalities—Winkie Pratney 10.99

Available in Salt Series

Available at bookstores everywhere or order direct from:
Huntington House Publishers • P.O. Box 53788 • Lafayette, LA 70505
Send check/money order. For faster service use VISA/MASTERCARD.
Call toll-free 1-800-749-4009.
Add: Freight and handling, $3.50 for the first book ordered, and $.50 for
each additional book up to 5 books.